Advance Praise for

Overcoming Reading Challenges

"A much-needed summary of what we know about supporting struggling readers. By unpacking key concepts related to literacy instruction and student agency, Vaughn and Massey strike a chord between empowering teachers and readers alike."
—Robin Griffith, PhD., Professor and Chair of
Department of Teaching and Learning Sciences,
Texas Christian University

"Using clear and digestible language, Vaughn and Massey's Overcoming Reading Challenges: Kindergarten through Middle School provides its readers with the mindsets and instructional moves they need to be effective literacy practitioners. With a focus on equity that helps bridge theory to practice, Vaughn and Massey's text serves both as a primer for those new to the field and a touchstone text for experienced teachers looking to engage with current research. I'm excited to use this compelling text with the pre-service teachers with whom I work, as well as the veteran teachers I help lead."
—Kyle Arlington, Superintendent of Kenilworth Schools, New Jersey

"Vaughn and Massey know that children are humans too. When so much of schooling focuses on measurement, achievement and accountability, Vaughn and Massey illustrate what we must know, but have sometimes forgotten, about the human element in literacy instruction: the roles of identity, and family and community, in raising a reader."
—Rachael Gabriel, PhD., Professor, Chair, of Literacy Instruction,
University of Connecticut

"Overcoming Reading Challenges: Kindergarten through Middle School" by Vaughn and Massey offers insight into how teachers can support children and youth who experience difficulties learning to read. Through easy-to-read chapters, the authors provide readers with nuance that can often be so difficult to capture in questions related to teaching reading and literacy research. "
—Sam DeJulio, Assistant Professor of Literacy, University of Texas at San Antonio

Overcoming Reading Challenges

Margaret Vaughn & Dixie D. Massey

Overcoming Reading Challenges

Kindergarten through Middle School

New York - Berlin - Bruxelles - Chennai - Lausanne - Oxford

Library of Congress Cataloging-in-Publication Data

Names: Vaughn, Margaret, author. | Massey, Dixie D., author.
Title: Overcoming reading challenges : kindergarten through middle school / Margaret Vaughn, Dixie Massey.
Description: New York : Peter Lang, 2024. | Includes bibliographical references and index.
Identifiers: LCCN 2023051285 (print) | LCCN 2023051286 (ebook) | ISBN 9781636671642 (paperback) | ISBN 9781636671659 (hardback) | ISBN 9781636670737 (pdf) | ISBN 9781636670744 (epub)
Subjects: LCSH: Reading (Elementary) | Reading (Middle school) | Reading–Remedial teaching. | Reading comprehension.
Classification: LCC LB1573 .V38 2024 (print) | LCC LB1573 (ebook) | DDC 372.4–dc23/eng/20231116
LC record available at https://lccn.loc.gov/2023051285
LC ebook record available at https://lccn.loc.gov/2023051286

DOI 10.3726/b21489

Bibliographic information published by the Deutsche Nationalbibliothek.
The German National Library lists this publication in the German National Bibliography; detailed bibliographic data is available on the Internet at http://dnb.d-nb.de.

Cover design by Peter Lang Group AG
ISBN 9781636671642 (paperback)
ISBN 9781636671659 (hardback)
ISBN 9781636670737 (ebook)
ISBN 9781636670744 (epub)
DOI 10.3726/b21489

© 2024 Peter Lang Group AG, Lausanne
Published by Peter Lang Publishing Inc., New York, USA
info@peterlang.com—www.peterlang.com

All rights reserved.

All parts of this publication are protected by copyright.

Any utilization outside the strict limits of the copyright law, without the permission of the publisher, is forbidden and liable to prosecution.
This applies in particular to reproductions, translations, microfilming, and storage and processing in electronic retrieval systems.

This publication has been peer reviewed.

Dedication
For Gerry Duffy and Sam Miller
whose mentorship and friendship continue to inspire us.

CONTENTS

List of figures/tables/images ix

Acknowledgments xi

Part I. Background

Chapter 1. When should a child be reading? 3

Chapter 2. What are the phases of reading development? 13

Chapter 3. How do you prepare for equitable reading instruction? 27

Chapter 4. What can a reader do and how can you use assessment to guide practice? 39

Part II. Dispositional

Chapter 5. How can you foster reading motivation? 55

Chapter 6. How can you support agentic readers? 71

Part III. Instructional approaches

Chapter 7. What can you do to strengthen phonemic awareness and phonics? 85

Chapter 8. What can you do to strengthen decoding and fluency? 97

Chapter 9. What can you do to strengthen students' comprehension and vocabulary? 107

Chapter 10. When a student starts middle school, now what? (disciplinary literacy) 127

Conclusion 145

Appendix A: Student interviews 151

Appendix B: Vocabulary plan 153

Index 157

LIST OF FIGURES/TABLES/IMAGES

Figures

Figure 2.1.	The Reader, Task, Text	15
Figure 4.1.	Information from Testing	41
Figure 4.2.	Assessment Framework	42
Figure 5.1.	Expectancy-Value Continuum of Motivation	56
Figure 7.1.	Relationship of Terms	86
Figure 9.1.	Four Levels of Vocabulary Knowledge	113
Figure 9.2.	Cup	114
Figure 9.3.	Conceptual Word Knowledge	115
Figure 9.4.	Comprehension Flowchart	116

Tables

Table 2.1.	Tasks of Reading	16
Table 2.2.	Receptive and Communicative Processes	16
Table 2.3.	Grade Level Differences in Readers, Texts, and Tasks	19
Table 3.1.	Ms. Hatkes Center Chart	29
Table 3.2.	Sample Picture Books and Comprehension Strategies	34

Table 3.3.	Common Difficulties	36
Table 4.1.	Observation Protocol	45
Table 4.2.	Challenges of Assessment in School	50
Table 5.1.	Challenges to Motivation in Reading in School	57
Table 5.2.	ABCDEs of Instruction to Encourage Motivation	58
Table 6.1.	Books to Discuss Agency	78
Table 7.1.	Books to Teach Skills	91
Table 8.1.	Sound-letter Relationships	100
Table 8.2.	Common Vowel Patterns	100
Table 8.3.	National Assessment of Educational Progress Fluency Scale	104
Table 9.1.	Challenges in Comprehension and Vocabulary	111
Table 9.2.	Text Structure	117
Table 10.1.	Common Core Standards Writing Goals for Elementary	130
Table 10.2.	Common Core Standards Writing Goals for Middle and Secondary	131
Table 10.3.	Challenges of Middle School Literacy	134
Table B.1.	Renewable and Nonrenewable Energy Concept Sort	154

Images

Image 1.1.	Leaf	6
Image 1.2.	Apples	7
Image 1.3.	Forest	8
Image 6.1.	Seventh Grade Reading Notebook	74
Image 6.2.	First Grade Reading Vision	75

ACKNOWLEDGMENTS

When we sat down to write this book, we were not alone. We want to thank the many students, teachers, and friends along the way who have taught us and continue to teach us in our lives. We want to especially thank our families, Mabel, Marcus, and Matthew (from Margaret) and Tori, Caleb, and Victor (from Dixie), who have supported us along as we wrote this book. Truth be told, this book would not have been written without their generous encouragement and support. And to our readers, thank you.

Part I
BACKGROUND

· 1 ·

WHEN SHOULD A CHILD BE READING?

In many districts across the US, kindergarten students are considered reading "at grade level expectations" if they enter kindergarten reading early reader books with sentences like, "Here is a cat." and "I see a dog." This expectation may exceed what you may think young readers should be able to do once they enter school. Some of you may think that young children entering school should primarily know the alphabet and how to count to twenty whereas some of you may think reading at this level is right on target. Who determines these benchmarks of when children should be reading in school? The answer to this question is more complex than you may think. In fact, literacy scholars have spent decades trying to answer this question. The quick answer is that national and state level educational policies directly inform student expectations and benchmarks for reading. Expectations of when children should be reading are high stakes for schools, parents, and children. If children are not reading on grade level reading they may be considered "at risk" with the recommendation for additional in-school services as well as remedial support out of school. Schools understand that a child who is considered a poor reader in first grade will most likely remain a poor reader at the end of fourth grade (Juel, 1988). Historically, educational reform efforts aimed at improving student literacy achievement outcomes for low-performing students who were not at benchmark flourished in the early 1990s and 2000s. In the 1990s, the US Congress approved the formation of the National Reading Panel (NRP) to outline effective, research-based instructional approaches to teaching reading (NICHD, 2000). The NRP reviewed the findings from the National Research Council which designated areas central to reading instruction: phonemic awareness, phonics instruction, fluency, comprehension, and vocabulary (Snow et al., 1998).

Based on these findings, the Reading First Initiative legislation in the US, within the No Child Left Behind Act (NCLB, 2001), was created. This initiative emphasized that all public school children in the US should read at or above grade level expectations by third grade. The Reading First Initiative defined scientifically-based research and outlined through the No Child Left Behind Act (NCLB, 2001) specific curricula and activities schools must use to teach reading. These literacy curricula programs had the five pillars of reading instruction outlined by the NRP (i.e., phonemic awareness, phonics, fluency, comprehension, and vocabulary). Schools had to adopt literacy curricula that was "scientifically-evidenced based" on these pillars and schools were required to only use research-based literacy curricula in schools in order to receive federal funding.

Schools across the nation were sent the message, "If it isn't proven to work through research, you can't count it toward instruction" (Manzo & Diegmueller, 2001, p. 5). In response to these initiatives, states and school districts increased accountability measures for schools and set in place measures to ensure that teachers taught these prescriptive literacy curricular programs to "fidelity" (Allington, 2013). What resulted for many teachers in schools across the US was increased pressure to adhere to standardized curricula at all costs and practices that emphasized "teaching to the test" to ensure that students performed adequately on state mandated literacy assessments.

Critical scholars emphasized that these scientifically-based research literacy programs lacked cultural relevance as well as engaging and authentic tasks and literature for students (Vaughn et al., 2022). In addition, teachers faced an extreme lack of autonomy because they were required to follow the script detailed in the lesson plan without any modification. As Allington (2010) counseled, "Such federal education policy during this time, adopted a narrow, ideologically defined notion of 'scientifically-based reliable reading research' and to date there is no compelling evidence that reading standards have improved as a result of NCLB" (p. 7). Literacy reform efforts continued with Race to the Top (Department of Education, 2009) where teachers received pay for performance scrutiny of their reading instruction (Vaughn et al., 2021).

Aggressive practices continued with the requirement of letter grades to schools state-wide according to their students' performances on standardized literacy assessments with state departments of education taking over schools considered "failing." With the Common Core State Standards (National Governors Association Center for Best Practices & Council of Chief State School Officers, 2010, CCSS), national standards were set in place to provide benchmark expectations of what students should be focused on per grade level and what expectations students should accomplish.

With these initiatives in place and because schools received federal funding for student performance on standardized assessment, teaching reading to children was considered (and continues to be) high stakes. For example, test scores are nationally and internationally populated (e.g., NAEP, PISA), and students are categorized according to their achievement indicators (at or above grade level). Results continue to quantify teacher and school performances, and state and federal funding are inextricably linked to the results. Educational reforms continue to rely on high stakes reading assessments which are tied to funding allocations to schools across the nation.

The question of when a child should be reading is indeed a complex question and not always connected to what we know about what works best for students. When you walk into most classrooms today, teachers are influenced either directly or indirectly by these past and current initiatives. For example, many teachers who are now teaching lived through NCLB and continue to adhere to a prescriptive curriculum to teach reading. This means that many of these teachers may align their instruction to meet the daily and weekly benchmarks of prescriptive, standardized curricula. Maybe that's not so bad, right? In some cases, and for some children, these programs work. However, what we know through careful research is that most standardized literacy programs rarely meet the individual and specific instructional needs of linguistically, racially diverse students as well as students from below the poverty line. Understanding how benchmarks inform such curricular programs is critical. Why are benchmarks evaluative when teaching reading?

What are benchmarks?

A benchmark is a standard that students are measured against. Typically, benchmark standards are established across the school year to show progress. Benchmarks can help us to outline our teaching goals, but we must be adaptive in our approach to teaching. There are student benchmarks for reading that are connected to the types of texts they read. For example, the Developmental Reading Assessment (Pearson Education, 2006) is an assessment that is often used to outline the reading level students should be reading according to their grade level across many schools.

According to this common benchmark guide, a child should be reading texts that look like the following image in the beginning of the school year in Kindergarten.

I see a leaf.

Image 1.1. Leaf

In order to successfully navigate this text, the reader has knowledge of the alphabetic principle, emerging phonological awareness, and beginning skills of how to decode. These concepts are discussed further in Chapters 7 and 8 but we briefly define these here:

- *Alphabetic principle*: the concept of how a child connects a letter to a specific sound. For example, the letter, "b" says "/bbb/ as in ball."
- *Phonological awareness*: the concept that outlines that sounds connect to words.
- *Decoding*: the ability to apply knowledge about letter and sound relationships to correctly pronounce and interpret a word.

A student who has reading difficulties with reading this type of text may be struggling with the alphabetic principle as well as having an emerging understanding of phonological awareness.

The role of assessment

As we discuss in Chapter 4, the role of assessment is critical in understanding a child's reading strategies and behaviors. We describe an assessment framework in this book that includes observation, conversation, and artifact/testing collection. Applied to early reading, we watch to see what a child does when reading or browsing books independently. Informal conversations help us understand what the child thinks about books and what books they might like—or if the child avoids books altogether. We also assess how children handle a book to help understand their experiences with books. Assessments like this includes asking the following questions:

1. Can you show me where a reader starts to read this book?

2. Where is the front and back of the book?

3. Can you find a word and put your fingers around a word chunk (i.e., "at")?

By asking these initial questions, we can find out about students' exposure to print and text. We also want to highlight the reading benchmark expected in first grade as outlined by the types of texts students are expected to read during this grade level. Here is what a first grader is expected to read when they *enter* first grade:

The apples are red.

Everyone wants to eat an apple.

Image 1.2. Apples

In this example, you can see that the sentences are varied with different sentence starters such as, "The apples are red," and, "Everyone wants to eat an apple." In this way, students are expected to look within words and use what they know about letter patterns to read the words like, "red," and "eat."

Now consider what a first grader is expected to read *by the end* of first grade. You can see the complexities associated with reading the text and the minimal picture clues to guide the reader when reading this particular text.

One day a little girl went walking in the woods. She saw a long trail. The trail was winding and had many plants and animals. The girl stopped and saw a tree that had a hole in it. She looked inside of the hole and saw a little squirrel and its family.

Image 1.3. Forest

As this example suggests, the reader must engage in more complex strategies. These include applying word knowledge, utilizing context clues, as well as comprehending what the story is about to make sense of what is read. Typically, students who experience reading difficulties with a text like this may be struggling with fluency, comprehension, and/or vocabulary. We briefly outline these concepts below but discuss these in depth in Chapters 8 and 9.

- *Fluency*: the ways in which a reader reads a text with expression, accuracy, and meaning

- *Comprehension*: how a reader interprets and understands what they read
- *Vocabulary*: the specific use of words in a text

We provide these examples of texts to showcase the benchmarks for reading in these sample grades as well as the complexities students must navigate when reading. We also emphasize the role of the teacher when teaching reading to help scaffold students as they read increasingly complex texts.

Setting the stage for reading

States, districts, and schools use benchmarks to help guide reading instruction. These guidelines help support our reading instructional goals for our students. We want to recognize the role of outlined benchmarks for students but also recognize that benchmarks alone are insufficient because no two students are alike. As teachers, we must approach teaching reading from an adaptive perspective (Vaughn et al., 2021, 2022), meaning that we must be flexible in our approach to teaching reading. We adjust our teaching to fit the specific, instructional needs of the students that we have in our classrooms.

Additionally, we must also work on supporting a reader's identity—which means they are supported beyond benchmarks. A reader's identity is how a student views his or her roles as a reader. This is inextricably linked to the culture about reading that is promoted in the classroom. The classroom community determines how reading is defined, instructed, and evaluated (Wenger, 2000). For example, many of you who are reading this book may be proficient and skilled readers. Others may not be. Why do you view your reading identity in this way? Maybe you enjoyed books or had a teacher who encouraged and supported you in your efforts to read? Perhaps you came from experiences where you had access to books and materials where reading was a part of your life. Or maybe you are reading this book because it is part of your required reading for a course or professional development. Maybe you dislike reading and would rather do something other than reading. For example, Margaret never liked to read as a child. She was painfully shy and during most of her reading instruction in school, the teacher practiced popcorn reading where students took turns reading a text passage out loud. She would get so caught up in when it was her turn, that she would forget her place and end up reading the wrong passage. She was then put in the "low level" reading group because it was believed that she could not read even though she could in fact read. This practice greatly discouraged her interest in books, and she didn't like reading until she graduated college and started reading books that interested and motivated her. Dixie, on the other hand, has been an avid reader from the moment she first cracked the code in kindergarten.

Just like us, our students have different background experiences with reading. What occurs in school can sometimes enhance or detract from supporting readers. As with Margaret, reading in school never quite worked for her; however, for Dixie it did. To develop readers, we must be flexible and adaptive in our approach to teaching reading while keeping in mind that reading instruction requires explicit instruction of skills.

What about parents?

For parents, messages about benchmarks and when their child should be reading can be very confusing and stressful. A question we often hear parents ask us, "How is it that my child is already considered behind in kindergarten?" We talk more about this phenomenon in Chapter 7 but provide context here. It is important to acknowledge to parents that as students enter our classroom, they come to us with different ideas, beliefs, strengths, and experiences with reading than our own as well as different experiences from one another. In fact, in our 20+ years of teaching reading, we have never found two readers who were exactly the same.

As much as we want to outline a time stamp on when a child should be reading on their own, they read at different times and phases. Our role as educators is to teach explicitly the necessary literacy skills (i.e., phonemic awareness, phonics, fluency, comprehension, and vocabulary) readers need while engaging them in texts and tasks that are interesting and culturally relevant. We believe that when we teach students these skills explicitly, we support their interest in reading as well as providing them with the necessary skills and strategies to engage meaningfully with texts. Sometimes this happens for students in a neat timeline and students progress through school with minimal struggle when it comes to reading. And sometimes, it doesn't happen that way despite our best efforts. For example, Margaret started reading to her son as soon as he was born. When he turned two, he wasn't much interested in books. As he turned four, five, and six years old, he still wasn't interested in reading books on his own. The day after he turned seven, a lightbulb went off and you could find him curled up with the latest graphic novel, *Dogman* (Pilkey, 2021) in his room. He was ready to read on his own when *he was ready* not on some predetermined benchmark. The explicit teaching of skills provided the structure and support he needed to launch him to reading on his own.

Many parents read with their children, talk about books, and engage in literacy practices at home that help to build the necessary support and strategies for their children to read. Our role as educators is to teach skills explicitly and provide access to engaging and culturally relevant and linguistically diverse materials so that students want to read. Families can assist us in this task by continuing to make reading fun and by providing the specific cultural components that support their family's identity.

How this book works

This book is organized by guiding questions that mark each chapter's title. Each chapter starts with this guiding question followed by related research, theory, and approaches to put these ideas into classroom practice. Each chapter provides reflective questions on ways to dig deeper with the theories and ideas presented in the chapter. We emphasize that reading is shaped by the culture of the classroom which helps to determine how reading is defined, instructed, and evaluated. We look at common reading difficulties children experience and strategies to support these challenges. We invite you to think deeply about the ideas and theories presented to reflect on the culture of reading you would like to support in your classroom. Let's get started!

Reflective questions

1. What are current local educational policies that are affecting your local school system? How do these educational policies connect to the reading practices in schools? If you aren't sure, how would you find out? What messages are sent out locally about current educational concerns?

2. Reflect on your own reading experiences in school. How was reading instruction and benchmarks for reading organized in school? How did this influence your view of yourself as a reader?

3. What types of texts are engaging for young readers-particularly at the kindergarten and first grade level? Preview a classroom library and find interesting, engaging, and culturally relevant texts that would invite young readers to read.

References

Allington, R. L. (2010). Recent federal education policy in the United States. In D. Wyse, R. Andrews, & J. V. Hoffman (Eds.), *The Routledge international handbook of English, language and literacy teaching* (pp. 496–507). Routledge.

Allington, R. L. (2013). What really matters when working with struggling readers. *The Reading Teacher, 66*(7), 520–530.

Department of Education. (2009). *Race to the top program executive summary*. US Department of Education.

Juel, C. (1988). Learning to read and write: A longitudinal study of 54 children from first to fourth grades. *Journal of Educational Psychology, 80*(4), 437–447.

Manzo, K. K., & Diegmueller, K. (2001). IRA attendees flock to sessions on applying reading research. *Education Week, 20*(34), 5.

National Governors Association Center for Best Practices & Council of Chief State School Officers. (2010). *Common Core State Standards for English language arts and literacy in history/social studies, science, and technical subjects*. Washington, DC: Authors.

National Institute of Child Health and Development (NICHD). (2000). Report of the National Reading Panel: Teaching children to read: An evidence-based assessment of the scientific research literature on reading and its implications for reading instruction (NIH Publication No. 00–4769). Washington, DC: U.S. Government Printing Office. Available at https://www.nichd.nih.gov/publications/pubs/nrp/pages/smallbook.aspx

No Child Left Behind (NCLB) Act of 2001, Pub. L. No. 107–110, § 115, Stat. 1425 (2002).

Pilkey, D. (2021). *Dogman* (series). Scholastic Inc.

Snow, C., Bums, M., & Griffin, P. (1998). *Preventing reading difficulties in young children*. Washington, DC: National Academy Press.

Vaughn, M., Parsons, S. A., & Gallagher, M. A. (2022). Challenging scripted curricula with adaptive teaching. *Educational Researcher, 51*(3), 186–196.

Vaughn, M., Scales, R. Q., Stevens, E., Kline, S., Barrett-Tatum, J., Van Wig, A., Yoder, K. K., & Wellman, D. (2021). Understanding literacy adoption policies across contexts: A multistate examination of literacy curriculum decision-making. *Journal of Curriculum Studies, 53*(3), 333–352.

Wenger, E. (2000). Communities of practice and social learning systems. *Organization, 7*(2), 225–246.

· 2 ·

WHAT ARE THE PHASES OF READING DEVELOPMENT?

Lalia, a first grader, was in a small reading group that was meeting with her teacher, Mr. Yates. Mr. Yates had divided the small group into partners and was listening to the partners read to one another. When Lalia came to the word "star," she paused, then read "silly." Mr. Yates could respond in several ways. He could praise Lalia for her attempt at the unknown word. He could wait and see if Lalia and her partner could decode the word. He could prompt Lalia to look again and see if the word makes sense. He could tell Lalia the word so that she could continue to read and not lose the flow of the story. He could pause and model how to decode the word. Each decision is appropriate, so how can he decide? He must make an in-the-moment decision based on his knowledge of Lalia, her partner, the text, and the objective of the lesson.

    In Chapter 1, we set the stage for a developmental perspective on teaching reading by looking at how texts in kindergarten and first grade require different reading knowledge and behaviors. In this chapter, we examine development that happens in the primary and intermediate grades. Development denotes something that happens over time. Development also suggests that it might not happen at the same time for everyone. Think about young children learning to walk. Some seemly can't wait to walk. Others are content to crawl or let the world go on around them. Pediatricians suggest that typically developing children will walk anytime between 8 and 18 months. What accounts for such a wide variation in learning to walk? Personality, older siblings, and so much more. Similarly, reading develops over time but at very different rates for children. Reading is also influenced by personality, interest, family dynamics, access, and more (Baker et al., 1997; Hidi, 2001; Medford & McGeown, 2012).

This willingness to take a developmental perspective on reading and to make differentiated decisions is why Mr. Yates responded in a particular way to Lalia. Because Mr. Yates knew that Lalia had been reluctant to try new words in the past and because he wanted her to attempt new words before appealing for help, he chose to praise her for her attempt. He coupled his praise with a mirror of what Lalia read. "Lalia, I am so proud of you for reading all of those words! Now, listen to me read what you just read and see if the sentence makes sense." Mr. Yates reread the sentence the way that Lalia read the sentence and she noted that it did not make sense but she could not find her error. Because the students were still working in pairs, Mr. Yates took a bit more time to model how to monitor comprehension and break the word star in the /st/ blend and the /ar/ patterns. No curriculum can account for all the unique differences in a single class, making it paramount that teachers develop a decision-making framework to guide their moment-by-moment thinking and foster a willingness to adapt the curriculum to specific children.

Research on developmental perspectives

We use the RAND Reading Study Group's (Snow, 2002) categories to provide entry points for instruction. These categories remind us to consider the readers, the tasks, the texts, the contexts (See Figure 2.1) as we plan instruction.

The readers

Research offers some big-picture ways of thinking about primary and intermediate grade readers. First, all readers are agentic. By agentic, we mean that readers make decisions, use what they know, and then take risks as they read. Readers are not just influenced by their environments and the information they are given, instead, they actively seek out information and opportunities. Psychologists have observed that infants as young as eight months selectively attend to certain objects and that they remain most attentive when the "sequence of objects that is neither too predictable nor too unpredictable, as

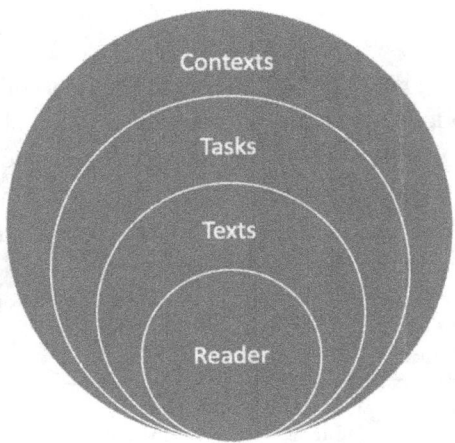

Figure 2.1. The Reader, Task, Text

if to say that they choose to attend to stimuli that are 'just right'" (Xu, 2019, p. 54). Xu referred to this as "child-as-an-active-learner."

> The child-as-an-active-learner claim captures the idea that development is an interplay between the child and her environment. Even as infants, the young learner chooses what to attend to, what to play with, who to learn from, and where to seek help. As the learner grows, she also learns to generate her own data, directly (as in manipulating the physical world) or indirectly (as in seeking explanations through question asking). In other words, cognitive agency is an integral part of a theory of development. (p. 56)

This is a critical part of understanding reading and readers. Just as infants are selectively attentive, our readers are also selectively attentive. We can give them all kinds of texts and tasks but if we are not attending to the alignment of their interests and attention with the tasks and texts, then they may be selectively turning their attention to other things.

While all readers are agentic and selective, some differences are related to development and age. For example, working memory increases with grade level (Peng et al., 2018). As children gain more experiences with their surroundings, linking those experiences requires less mental effort, allowing them more cognitive space to focus on other things such as making meaning, drawing inferences, and monitoring their own understanding (Bjorklund, 1987). It may seem obvious, but readers, their decision-making processes, interests, and abilities are critical when thinking about reading instruction.

The tasks

The National Reading Panel (2000) identified five main pillars of reading: phonemic awareness, phonics, vocabulary, fluency, and vocabulary. These pillars can be considered the topics of learning to read. Each topic can include specific tasks. For example, phonics includes tasks such as learning common patterns (e.g., blends, digraphs, long vowel patterns). Comprehension tasks include summarizing a text, monitoring one's understanding, and participating in a discussion about the text. A sampling of additional tasks is listed in Table 2.1.

Table 2.1. Tasks of Reading

Phonemic Awareness	Phonics	Fluency	Vocabulary	Comprehension
Rhyming sounds Blending sounds Segmenting sounds Awareness of words Awareness of letters of the alphabet	Solidifying letter name to sound link Representing sounds with letters in writing Decoding words by recognizing patterns (blends, digraphs, vowel patterns)	Identifying words with automaticity Reading with a variable rate Reading with appropriate prosody/phrasing to support meaning of phrases instead of individual words Reading with appropriate expression to support meaning	Developing background knowledge in disciplines (math, science, etc.) Recognizing sound/spelling links to meaning through roots and affixes Gaining syntactic knowledge of language	Developing background knowledge in disciplines (math, science, etc.) and with texts Using patterns (genres) of texts to identify questions Using patterns of thinking (summarizing, connecting, inferring, questioning) to make sense of text

The tasks listed in this table focus on the primary elements of reading. However, students are expected to do much more than read. The International Literacy Association defines literacy as three dyads: reading/writing; speaking/listening; and viewing/composing. These dyads have a receptive component (reading, listening, viewing—shown in bold in Table 2.2) where the students take in information. They also include a communicative component (writing, speaking, composing—shown in italics in Table 2.2) where the student is asked to communicate information in a written, verbal, or visual way.

Table 2.2. Receptive and Communicative Processes

Reading	**Listening**	**Viewing**
Writing	*Speaking*	*Composing*

Communicative tasks include speaking, writing, and composing. Within each of these areas, the specific tasks are limitless and may also come in combination. For example, students may be asked to participate in a book club where they are expected to speak about the text and collaboratively develop a presentation about the text.

Some students may be stronger at the receptive tasks than the communicative tasks. The reverse can also be true: some students are strong communicators, and they may use that to get additional help with the cognitive tasks.

Many of the tasks that you will give students will be identified by a curriculum. We encourage you to evaluate these tasks carefully, making sure that one type of task is not over-emphasized or neglected. For example, we see many curricula emphasize the receptive tasks over the communicative tasks. Communicative tasks often take longer for students to complete than receptive tasks, and yet we need students who are not just receivers of information but can communicate the information to others as well.

In addition to considering if one particular task is being over or under-emphasized, consider students' motivation for the tasks. Different types of instructional tasks influence students' motivation to learn (Brophy, 1983). Academic tasks that are authentic and engaging encourage students to value the process of learning. These types of tasks support students' willingness to participate and engage in the learning process. Authentic tasks include tasks that replicate real-world situations such as book clubs and tasks that are open-ended and allow students to make choices. Moreover, tasks should be structured to help increase students' motivation. We will talk more about the important role of motivation in Chapter 5 but emphasize motivation is central within the tasks we structure to engage students in reading.

The texts

Readers encounter certain kinds of texts in their elementary years. We can group texts into a few broad categories:

- Decodable texts. These texts are meant to help students practice patterns that are phonetically regular. For example, a decodable text that helps students practice the short /a/ vowel pattern might have a sentence such as, "The fat cat sat on the mat." Decodables will include

high frequency words such as, the, on, and it. Sentences will build on previously learned vowel patterns.
- Pattern texts. These texts are written with repetitive patterns. For example, *Brown Bear, Brown Bear* (Martin & Carle, 1984) is a pattern book. Students will encounter words that are beyond the phonics patterns that they recognize, such as purple in *Brown Bear*. However, because of the pattern and the picture support, they are able to identify the words.
- Leveled texts. There are many different leveling systems that use letters, numbers, or Lexile scores. Leveling is based on considerations of the length of the sentence and the number of syllables within the words. More complex leveling systems will also include a more subjective analysis of the topic of the text, with texts that deal with death or tragedy being labeled with a higher level even if the words and sentences might be easily understood by those reading at lower levels.
- Trade books. A trade book is a general term for books that are published by a commercial publisher and are intended for general readers. Decodable texts are not considered trade books while the *Lunch Lady* (Krosoczka, 2009) books are considered trade books. Chapter books are considered trade books.
- Curricular texts. Students are likely to encounter anthologies or texts collected within a larger text. These curricular texts may include stories that are written to go with the curricular theme. They may also be excerpts from longer works.
- Narrative, Expository, and Poetic Texts. Many schools use the terms fiction and nonfiction texts. We prefer to use narrative, expository, and poetic. Narrative texts are those that tell a story. They have characters, settings, and problems. A narrative text can be fiction or nonfiction. For example, a memoir is nonfiction. It is also a narrative. Expository texts are those texts that are nonfiction and that are written about a topic rather than a character. Texts about hurricanes or the 13 colonies are typically written as expository texts. We believe it is important to distinguish narrative from expository because it is important that students encounter both fiction and nonfiction texts, and that they are encountering different text formats. Poetic texts may be collections of poems or connected poems that form a narrative and tell a true or made-up story. In the past, some curricula offered texts that included an over-emphasis on narrative. Students read fictional narratives about children and animals; they also read nonfictional narratives about specific people. While

they were getting both fiction and nonfiction texts, they were unprepared to read an expository text for science or social studies.

Many texts do not fit clearly into a single category. For example, graphic novels can include both narrative and expository elements. Texts such as *Crossover* (Alexander, 2017) are written in free-verse poetry but also tell a narrative story. We leave the categorization of books to librarians, or you can view our book on children's literature (Vaughn & Massey, 2021). Our focus centers on giving students access to a wide range of texts that include all these divisions.

Additionally, we think broadly about what counts as text. As stated in the ILA definition, reading requires a multitude of skills that extends beyond printed text. Online texts such as a webpage may include a visual component such as a diagram or map, a written component such as text, and an embedded video. It is important that elementary students learn how to navigate these kinds of texts also, including how to search, evaluate, and discern important information. In other words, when asked what students should be reading, our answer is "Everything that is age appropriate!" Table 2.3 summarizes some of the differences for readers, texts, and tasks in primary and intermediate readers.

Table 2.3. Grade Level Differences in Readers, Texts, and Tasks

Primary (K-2)	Intermediate (3–5)
Limited working memory; more mental energy needed to make connections, decode words, identify vocabulary	Increasing vocabulary and experiences allow more mental energy towards sense-making; greater opportunities for more complex inferences and connections to background knowledge
Emphasis on topics of phonemic awareness, phonics, and fluency while developing vocabulary and comprehension	Emphasis on vocabulary and comprehension, sometimes called reading for learning
Emphasis on decodable texts, pattern texts, and trade books	Emphasis on trade books and texts across genres

The contexts

Context is the final component. Although we often think of literacy as a set of all-purpose skills and strategies to be learned, it is more complex, local, personal, and social than that. Becoming literate involves developing strong reading identities, relationships, dispositions, and values as much as acquiring strategies and skills for working with texts (Vaughn & Massey, 2021). These are influenced by a variety of contexts, such as home, school, and community.

As teachers, our job is to explicitly teach the skills and strategies of reading as we recognize and honor students' contexts, backgrounds, and prior experiences. Additionally, we teach skills and strategies not just so that students can achieve certain scores. We teach skills and strategies so that students can participate with others in society (Freebody & Luke, 1990). Reading literature needs to be viewed in its full range of contexts—not just cognitive—but social and cultural as well (Gee, 2015).

What's important about a development approach to reading?

One of the most important things about recognizing that students are on a developmental progression is acknowledging that development means no two children will be at exactly the same place at the same time. Just as doctors have expected ranges for height, weight, and physical milestones, there are ranges of reading progression. These are usually expressed in the state standards or objectives.

Not every state follows the Common Core State Standards (National Governors Association Center for Best Practices & Council of Chief State School Officers, 2010). However, most states have standards that expect students to demonstrate similar proficiency. Let's look at a few of those standards related to reading literature:

- Kindergarten: With prompting and support, ask and answer questions about key details in a text.
- Third grade: Ask and answer questions to demonstrate understanding of a text, referring explicitly to the text as the basis for the answers.
- Fifth grade: Quote accurately from a text when explaining what the text says explicitly and when drawing inferences from the text.

These standards offer an expected range of development. In kindergarten, children respond to questions about important parts of a text. By fifth grade, students should be able to identify what is important and to reference and quote from a text.

What about the students who are falling behind?

Temple Grandin, author of *The Autistic Brain* (Grandin, 2014) and herself a person with autism, describes her own development as delayed when compared with her peers. She did not learn to speak until she was four and did not read until she was eight, yet she went on to earn a PhD and become a professor, author, and public speaker. Even though she did learn to speak, read, and write, she wrote that language is still not the primary way she takes in information. When describing her development, she explained:

> These days, "neurotypical" has replaced the term "normal." Neurotypicals are generally described as people whose development happens in predictable ways at predictable times. It's a term that I shy away from, because defining what is neurotypical is as unhelpful as saying the average size of a dog. What's typical: A Chihuahua or a Great Dane? When does a little geeky or nerdy become autistic? When does distractible become ADHD, or when does a little moody become bipolar? These are all continuous traits. (Grandin, 2022, p. 35)

The point we want to emphasize is that there is no specific test or measure that identifies a child as falling behind in reading. It is not a binary but a continuum.

Earlier in the chapter, we used the acceptable range of learning to walk according to pediatricians as an example of the variability we can also expect in children learning to read. In medicine, "Failure to Thrive," is the label given when children or teens have a significantly lower rate of weight gain than other children or teens of similar age and sex. Doctors emphasize that it is not the actual weight but the rate of weight gain that can be most concerning. This is an excellent lens with which to view reading development. What is the rate of progression through the phases when compared to their peers—that is, other children in the same grade at the same school? In Temple Grandin's case, her parents and doctors recognized that her rate of learning to speak and read was much slower than other peers. What a developmental approach offers is a way to recognize what might come next. Even students who are developing at a slower rate will still need to learn to access the alphabetic code. They may need more time and additionally pedagogic approaches, but typically they will still move through the different phases of reading development. Grandin described her own process as one where she needed more time, intensive instruction with phonics, and tutoring to help her learn to read.

For those students who do need intervention, Spear-Swerling (2015) summarized three profiles of children struggling to read. Some children demonstrate word-recognition difficulties. Others exhibit reading-comprehension difficulties. Still others present a combination or mixed reading difficulties. The profile helps teachers with those students who are struggling and how they may need word level intervention, comprehension intervention, or a combination.

Teachers as decision-makers

We opened this chapter with Mr. Yates helping Lalia and her partner identify a word. This is an example of decision-making (Griffith, 2022) and decisions are an important part of teaching children to read. Effective decisions must be based on teacher knowledge (Griffith & Lacina, 2017). There are different types of knowledge, including knowledge of content or what is to be taught, knowledge of pedagogy or how to teach, knowledge of content pedagogy or how to teach the content to others, knowledge of the learner, and knowledge of the goals and objectives for teaching.

When it comes to knowing the learner, we need to make sure that our knowledge is based on a variety of information and not just a few scores from specific tests. We encourage teachers to collect their own data through an assessment framework that you will see repeated in this book: observations, conversations, and artifacts/testing. Create a full portrait of the student before raising any alarms. Additionally, talk with the student, and family members, and learn all you can about the student. Talk with other professionals in the school. Ultimately, you will decide based on all the information that you have.

Teacher decisions are a critical part of a developmental perspective. By making small decisions that are not necessarily the same for each student, we acknowledge that each student is different. While one student may benefit from praise over an attempt, another student will need a more explicit model. Understanding developmental progression means we own the responsibility to adapt our teaching to make the best decision we can in-the-moment (Parsons & Vaughn, 2021).

In another classroom, for example, Ms. Jones was also faced with important decisions. She was worried about four of her students who did not seem to be progressing. While many of her third graders were comfortable reading chapter books, these four preferred picture books, comics, and graphic novels. Each of them received some pull-out services. While this was helping their decoding and fluency skills, she worried that it was also labeling them as different from others in the class.

Ms. Jones decided to use her flexible small group time to work with the four students and have them perform reader's theater, a practice where students reread a script and then perform the same script. She had not yet used reader's theater with the class, and she thought this would be a good opportunity to model. She chose to invite these four students so that she could elevate their status as readers and classroom participants. By getting to do something that no other group of students had done, she hoped that they would be viewed as the experts.

Across four weeks, she helped these four readers practice two separate short scripts and perform for the class. Because they were rereading familiar scripts, the four readers read fluently like other readers in the class. Because she purposefully wrote scripts from picture books that were engaging, the four students were viewed as entertainers. She assured the rest of the class that they would also get to participate in reader's theater. She asked her four readers to share tips about what they were learning about performing reader's theater.

Ms. Jones' as well as Mr. Yate's (from the beginning of the chapter) and their actions acknowledged that students develop reading skills over time. Phases of reading development remind us that students' literacy abilities develop at different rates across time. Taking a developmental approach helps remind us that one size doesn't fit all. We need to be thoughtful decision makers and adapt to the specific and individual students in front of us.

Reflective questions

1. When thinking of the image of Reader/Texts/Tasks/Contexts/what might happen if one of the circles became too small/too big? How might this figure get out of balance and what would you do?

2. Would your decisions change if the grade levels were reversed in the case studies? If Ms. Jones taught first grade and Mr. Yates taught third grade, would your decisions change? Why and How?

3. How did Mr. Yates and Ms. Jones' decisions reflect a developmental perspective on teaching reading and how did these decisions support students' reading identities?

References

Alexander, K. (2017). *The crossover*. Albin Michel.

Baker, L., Scher, D., & Mackler, K. (1997). Home and family influences on motivations for reading. *Educational Psychologist, 32*(2), 69–82.

Bjorklund, D. F. (1987). How age changes in knowledge base contribute to the development of children's memory: An interpretive review. *Developmental Review, 7*(2), 93–130.

Brophy, J. (1983). Conceptualizing student motivation. *Educational Psychologist, 18*(3), 200–215.

Freebody, P., & Luke, A. (1990). Literacies programs: Debates and demands in cultural context. *Prospect, 5*(3), 85–94.

Gee, J. (2015). The new literacy studies. In J. Rowsell & K. Pahl (Eds.), *The Routledge handbook of literacy studies* (pp. 35–48). Routledge.

Grandin, T. (2014). *The autistic brain*. Mariner Books.

Grandin, T. (2022). *Visual thinking*. Riverhead Books.

Griffith, R. (2022). *Teachers as decision makers: Responsive guided reading instruction* Stenhouse.

Griffith, R., & Lacina, J. (2017). Teacher as decision maker: A framework to guide teaching decisions in reading. *The Reading Teacher, 71*, 501–507.

Hidi, S. (2001). Interest, reading, and learning: Theoretical and practical considerations. *Educational Psychology Review, 13*, 191–209.

Krosoczka, J. J. (2009). *Lunch Lady and the league of librarians: Lunch Lady# 2* (Vol. 2). Knopf Books for Young Readers.

Martin, B., & Carle, E. (1984). *Brown bear, brown bear*. Puffin books.

Medford, E., & McGeown, S. P. (2012). The influence of personality characteristics on children's intrinsic reading motivation. *Learning and Individual Differences, 22*(6), 786–791.

National Governors Association Center for Best Practices & Council of Chief State School Officers. (2010). *Common Core State Standards for English language arts and literacy in history/social studies, science, and technical subjects*. Washington, DC: Authors.

National Reading Panel (US), National Institute of Child Health, & Human Development (US). (2000). *Teaching children to read: An evidence-based assessment of the scientific research literature on reading and its implications for reading instruction: Reports of the subgroups*. National Institute of Child Health and Human Development, National Institutes of Health.

Parsons, S. A., & Vaughn, M. (Eds.). (2021). *Principles of effective literacy instruction, K-5*. Guilford Press.

Peng, P., Barnes, M., Wang, C., Wang, W., Li, S., Swanson, H. L., & Tao, S. (2018). A meta-analysis on the relation between reading and working memory. *Psychological Bulletin, 144*(1), 48.

Snow, C. (2002). *Reading for understanding: Toward an R&D program in reading comprehension*. Rand Corporation.

Spear-Swerling, L. (2015). A bridge too far?: Implications of the Common Core for students with different kinds of reading problems. *Perspectives on Language and Literacy, 41*(2), 25–30.

Vaughn, M., & Massey, D. (2021). *Teaching with children's literature: Theory to practice.* Guilford Press.

Xu, F. (2019). Towards a rational constructivist theory of cognitive development. *Psychology Review, 126,* 841–864.

· 3 ·

HOW DO YOU PREPARE FOR EQUITABLE READING INSTRUCTION?

What is equitable reading instruction? Equitable reading instruction involves viewing students as knowledgeable meaning makers who possess skills and knowledge essential to classroom learning. Equitable reading instruction is based on a strength-based approach to viewing students as opposed to viewing students from a deficit-based approach. This means that students and families' cultures, languages, and experiences are welcome and essential components of classroom instruction. Teachers must be adaptive and center their instruction in ways that support students' cultural and linguistic backgrounds as well as focus on strengthening instructional skills. In this chapter, we explore what equitable reading instruction looks like through the types of texts readers should read to the need for a comprehensive instructional approach to reading that is rooted in what we know from research on effective reading instruction.

Research on equitable reading instruction

Equitable and effective reading instruction relies on embedding literacy instruction within culturally responsive frames of teaching. Culturally responsive teaching ensures that teachers "take the cultural knowledge, prior experiences, frames of reference and performance styles of ethnically diverse students to make learning encounters more relevant to and effective for [students]" (Gay, 2018, p. 29). Moreover, culturally responsive teaching requires that teachers view students as knowledgeable meaning makers who have the necessary skills and knowledge to be vital contributors in the learning process. Such a view aligns with a funds of knowledge approach (Moll et al., 1992) where the knowledge and expertise students have because of their language, experiences, and cultures are valued. This approach acknowledges that students and families are generative and meaningful partners in the classroom. Effective and equitable reading instruction views students from this strength-based perspective.

High quality materials that are culturally responsive such as the types of texts teachers use in classrooms are crucial to structuring equitable reading classroom spaces. Because culturally responsive teaching centers instruction on organizing instruction on meeting students' linguistic and cultural needs, teachers of reading must utilize this approach when planning for equitable reading instruction. This means a variety of things from selecting texts that provide accurate portrayals of historically underrepresented individuals and communities as well as encouraging the use of students' first language when reading and speaking in school.

Teaching reading equitably relies on knowledge of effective reading instruction. Effective reading teachers support their students by knowing their content. That is, teachers must possess the knowledge and skills required to teach various aspects of reading. In addition, teachers are reflective and receptive to learning about their students. For example, effective teachers understand that the role of assessment is crucial for determining instruction when students experience difficulties when it comes to reading. The valuable role of assessment cannot be undermined when we think about planning for effective reading instruction. As we outline in Chapter 4, equitable reading instruction is guided by assessment where teachers assess in various ways the dimensions of reading (e.g., phonemic awareness, morphological knowledge, etc.).

Additionally, we know that effective reading instruction is guided by a flexible and adaptive approach to teaching reading. For example, in their nationwide study of effective reading teachers from first and fourth grade across the nation, Pressley and colleagues (1998, 2001) found that the most effective reading teachers used multiple strategies when teaching literacy skills and were flexible in their approach to teaching reading. In other words, the most effective reading teachers were *adaptive* in their approach to teaching reading. A singular curricular program was not the missing ingredient to achieving reading growth in students but rather these teachers used a variety of strategies, tasks,

HOW DO YOU PREPARE FOR EQUITABLE READING INSTRUCTION?

and materials. As we think about adaptive and effective reading instruction, what exactly do effective teachers of reading do?

Some important characteristics of effective literacy teachers as outlined in Allington's (2002) decade-long research in schools includes: the 6 T's of effective teaching including: *time* for students to read, *texts* that are engaging, *teaching* that is flexible and adaptive, *talk* that engages students in higher-level thinking, *tasks* that are authentic and engaging, and *testing*. Importantly, effective reading teachers balance reading and writing tasks in their classrooms to provide opportunities for students to read and engage in writing for authentic and meaningful purposes.

Instruction on equitable reading instruction

Effective teaching equals equitable reading instruction. Consider the following scenario of how Ms. Hatkes, a first grade teacher, puts these elements into practice during her 60 minute reading block where she conducts guided reading instruction and students work in centers (Table 3.1).

Table 3.1. Ms. Hatkes Center Chart

*Students' Names Group A	Group B	Group C	Group D
Topic Baskets	Student Project	Reading Center	Art Center
Science Center	Computer Center	Student Project	Vocabulary
Math Center	Buddy Reading	Math tubs	Student Project
Student Project	Writing Center	Audiobooks	Math skills

*Students are in heterogeneous groups and these groups should change out biweekly

Each day, students go to their respective centers as outlined. These centers include a variety of high challenge tasks from Topic baskets where students are encouraged to explore, read, and write about a particular topic they choose. Topic baskets are labeled with a variety of reading materials. One basket is labeled as engineering, and within this basket, there are manuals, books about what an engineer does, and also a task for students to build and create. In other tubs, (e.g., math tubs, math skills), students have a variety of math tasks to complete and write about in their math journal. Students practice reading and writing in various ways from buddy reading where they read with a friend, to the Reading center where they can explore any books of their choosing. When students go to the Writing center, they are encouraged to work on their story from their writing notebook or explore other writing materials to create a new book, draft a letter to a friend, or interview a friend about something they are interested in and want to learn. In another center, the Student project, students meet with their teacher to outline a research project of their choice at the beginning of the month. One group of students works to organize a gently used book drive in the school. Another group wants to restore the nature trail outside of the school. Students work on tasks for these self-selected projects during center time. For example, for the book drive, the students create a checklist including who to talk with and how to write a clear purpose for their project. Center activities change typically biweekly, and students are taught how to participate and use the materials in the centers to ensure that students can be successful.

Because students are actively engaged in doing their centers, Ms. Hatkes can work with small groups of students to focus on targeted reading skills during guided reading instruction. Guided reading instruction centers on the teacher working with a small group of students on specific, targeted reading skills. Students are actively involved in their center work when not meeting with Ms. Hatkes. Like this, there are several organizational structures you can use to organize your classroom. We list some approaches here that can guide you as you think of how to provide equitable reading instruction to align with Allington's (2002) aforementioned 6T's (i.e., time, texts, teaching, talking, tasks, and testing).

Workshop

The workshop approach (Atwell, 2007) centers on a whole group modeling of a targeted reading/ writing skill. The teacher models the skill for the whole group and then practices the skill with students before tasking students to work on the skill independently. The modeling is formatted to front load an explicit targeted skill. The teacher models, then students practice this skill as the teacher assesses and conferences with students. The class then discusses the targeted reading strategy that was modeled or anything else that developed as a result of the workshop for the day.

Daily Five

The Daily Five (Boushey & Moser, 2014) provides a way for students to practice authentic skills and affords an opportunity for the teacher to work with students in small groups. Students select from five authentic reading and writing choices, working independently toward personalized goals, while the teacher meets individual needs through whole-group and small-group instruction, as well as one-on-one conferring. These choices include:

- Read to Self
- Work on Writing (word stamps, writing stories from Writer's Workshop)
- Read to Someone
- Listen to Reading (computers)
- Word Work (could be using magnetic letters, or sorting smaller parts of words to practice morphological skills).

Café

The Café method (Boushey & Behne, 2019) is a method of reading instruction that focuses on comprehension, accuracy, fluency, and expanding vocabulary. Much like the workshop method, the teacher introduces the topic to the whole group and then students use these strategies as they read. The teacher works with small groups or with individual students to assess and monitor students.

Any of these approaches work with students and can support applying what we know about effective and equitable reading instruction (i.e., time, texts, teaching, talking, tasks, and testing) but the focus should be on explicit teaching of targeted skills. We recommend beginning with a model that you are comfortable with and then experimenting to see what aspects work for your specific group of students. By practicing how students should engage in any of the practices (e.g., read to self, work on writing, etc.), students will know behavior expectations. How will you choose which approach will work? We suggest creating a vision for teaching reading.

Visioning

Effective literacy teachers possess a vision of what it is they wish to accomplish in their work. A vision is, "an ideal image of classroom practice," (Hammerness, 2004), and an, "internal guiding system" (Corno, 2004). Visions reflect an image of what could be while presenting us with opportunities to reflect on how to attain our goals. Visioning serves as a compass and allows for us to take a careful look at ourselves, beliefs, and future goals (Duffy, 2002). Teachers who are effective and thoughtful in their approach to teaching reading, possess a vision for their classroom and their students.

What is your vision? We ask this question to the teachers we work with and are sometimes met with blank stares. So, we want to provide some sample questions to think about when conceptualizing your vision. We then provide some sample vision statements from effective teachers we know and work with but emphasize that there is no one correct vision. Visions are personal beliefs of what it is *you* want to accomplish with *your* teaching.

Questions to ask to develop your vision

1. What is it that you ultimately want for your students to be able to do when it comes to reading/writing? Why is this important to you and for your students?

2. What do you want for yourself as a teacher of reading? What is it that you ultimately want to be able to do when it comes to teaching your students?

Sample vision statements

- My vision for teaching reading is to create readers who have the necessary skills and interest in wanting to read-not just for what they are reading in school but reading outside of school too. I want them to see that reading is meaningful (first grade teacher).
- I want to be the kind of reading teacher that inspires my students to want to read any and everything. Ultimately, I want to teach my students that reading can be engaging and rewarding! (second grade teacher)
- My vision for teaching reading is that my students develop the skills of fluency and comprehension because they need that to be able to succeed in reading in fourth grade. (fourth grade teacher).
- My vision is for my students to learn how to find resources and materials on their own so that they can pursue their interests and ideas on their own. (fifth grade teacher).

Possessing a vision is particularly important in today's schools. Continually, teachers are faced with increased pressures to teach reading from a prescriptive and formulaic approach. As we shared in Chapter 1, teaching explicitly the essential skills of reading (i.e., phonics, fluency, vocabulary, comprehension, etc.) is indeed critical. Teachers can and should teach these explicit and necessary skills but if your vision is to create motivated readers who develop interest in reading, then teaching explicit skills should be done by including authentic and engaging materials (e.g., high interest texts, challenging tasks such as creating a multimodal book trailer) reflective of students' interests and choice and not through a worksheet, for example.

If your vision is to create motivated readers who develop interest in reading while possessing the necessary skills to read, what might your reading instruction might look like? To meet these aspects of your vision, your classroom should have a variety of texts that are culturally responsive as well as high-interest and engaging for your students. Within this classroom, you may adopt a gradual release of responsibility (Pearson & Gallagher, 1983) approach where you model explicit skills such as comprehension and use a variety of strategies. After modeling through mentor texts and guided practice, students then read and practice these strategies to master the modeled skills. In this classroom, students are taught strategies on how to self-select a text and are encouraged to read texts across a variety of genres. The classroom is organized where students have access to a wide variety of texts and are encouraged to explore reading materials throughout the day and at their own pace.

In this way, the teacher is strategic in her approach to structuring her classroom and her reading instruction to meet the aspects of her vision. To develop motivated readers, she provides opportunities where students actively engage in reading texts of their own choosing as well as flexible opportunities where students are encouraged to read a wide variety of texts. To support the necessary skills her readers need, she explicitly models a variety of strategies with literature that supports a particular skill that she is teaching.

Recently, we saw such a classroom where this occurred. The second grade teacher was modeling how readers ask questions to more readily engage and understand the author's purpose using the text, *What if* (Browne, 2014). In this text, the boy in the story asks questions using the prompt, what if, throughout the story and guides the reader on just how to engage with a text and the value of questioning as a comprehension strategy. The teacher maximized student engagement and interest by reading a wide variety of texts to support comprehension strategies during the week, modeling explicitly the skill of questioning.

This teacher understands that her vision guides her instructional decisions. Although in her school she has a prescriptive curriculum, she supplements her reading instruction by including high-interest and engaging texts like the ones

Table 3.2. Sample Picture Books and Comprehension Strategies

Title	Comprehension Strategy
The Proudest Blue by Ibtihaj Muhammed	Inferencing
Black is a Rainbow Color by Angela Joy	Making connections
Name Jar by Yangsook Choi	Questioning
El Deafo by Cece Bell	Visualizing
A Chair for my Mother by Vera B. Williams	Sequencing
111 Trees: How One Village Celebrates the Birth of Every Girl By Rina Singh	Synthesizing

outlined in Table 3.2 while also including multiple opportunities during the day where she encourages her students to read based on their interests.

The teacher is adaptive when teaching reading and selects aspects of the curriculum she thinks will support her students' instructional needs while modifying her reading instruction to support student engagement. Her vision guides her to make these instructional moves. In fact, when asked about her vision, she shared, "My vision is to create enthusiastic readers who can see themselves in what they read and who have the skills they need to attack and read anything they want to read."

As this vision suggests, visions represent our experiences as teachers and the knowledge we have on what works best for our students. Visions are guided by our knowledge of effective pedagogy, knowledge of students, and how to adapt our instruction to meet the specific instructional, cultural, and linguistic needs of our students. Teachers must engage in critical and careful reflection of their practice to ensure these aspects of their visions are met daily in their instructional practices.

Critical reflection of instructional practices provides a self-assessment mechanism of our practice to ensure that we are meeting the specific instructional needs of our students. Consider an example of our reflection from our teaching. When she was a first grade teacher, Margaret reflected on how she needed to embed more time in the schedule for her students to write so as to develop the skills of real writers. She reflected on what worked for students when it came to reading: self-selection of texts, time to collaborate with others, while receiving scaffolded support from her of explicit skills. Without carefully reflecting on what was needed next for her students as well as what was working (i.e., reading instruction, reading practices in the classroom), she would have missed ways to develop and enhance what she believed was missing in her classroom (i.e., explicit writing instruction in authentic and meaningful ways). Critical reflection is perhaps one of the most essential aspects of becoming an effective reading teacher and meeting the needs of all students.

On critical reflection

A simple way to begin engaging in critical reflection is to ask yourself before you teach a lesson, does this lesson align with my vision for my students? How will I reach all of the needs of my students? After you teach the lesson, reflect on what worked and what didn't and then make adjustments for the next lesson.

Consider again Ms. Hatkes, who was previously mentioned. During instruction, she noticed that students were not interested in editing their work. As soon as they finished a writing piece, they wanted to skip editing and advance to the publishing phase, so that they could read it to the whole class as part of the publishing party ritual. She decided to ask a few students about the process and when they told her that they just liked sharing their stories, she researched, talked with other teachers, and carefully reflected on her practice. What could she do to encourage collaborative learning while also encouraging students to review and edit their work? She tried a few different practices- from a whole group class discussion on the importance of editing to working with small groups on the editing process. After continual reflection, she came up with a few different strategies that she put in place. First, she worked with students to create a peer editing rubric. She modeled with students how to use the rubric. She also modeled discussion starters about student work that students could use when discussing stories, such as "One thing I noticed about your writing piece and one thing I wonder if you could build on in your story is . . ." Then she took time with students to model and scaffold these practices during writing time. She continually reflected on which students she could meet with individually to reteach strategies. In this way, critical reflection was essential to not only student learning but also whole class organization and management. What are some common difficulties in implementing the principles of equitable reading instruction? We outline these in the table (Table 3.3).

You can expect difficulties like those outlined in implementing the principles of equitable reading instruction. We have listed a few, along with some suggestions. In addition, we highly recommend working with other teachers at your school to work to make changes toward equitable reading instruction.

Table 3.3. Common Difficulties

Difficulty	Strategies to Overcoming These Difficulties
Teachers may be restricted by rigid schedules, district-wide prescriptive curricula that may/may not meet your individual students' needs, as well as a lack of funds to purchase texts.	Volunteer to serve on the scheduling committee and talk with other teachers about the need for targeted time for literacy instruction. Engage in conversations with other teachers about what works and what doesn't about the adopted curricula. Share these findings with literacy coaches, principals, and others. Serve on the literacy curricula adoption committee and present your findings. Work with local organizations to see about donating gently used books as well as asking for donations to a school book fund.
Classroom management tensions arise when trying to implement independent reading practices where students have more agency and control in what they are doing.	Talk with others about how they are managing their classroom to support independent reading time. Try to learn about ways teachers are supporting students to read on their own and to engage in self-directing opportunities to guide their learning.
Banning books that provide multiple representations.	Unfortunately, we are seeing a rise in the practice of banning books in schools across the nation. Talk with the school board and other officials in your community about the need for diverse books in your school and community.

This may include making decisions about scheduling, providing a voice in what curricula should be adopted, and sharing ideas on how to create safe spaces where students have the agency to read about their interests and see multiple representations of individuals and communities in the books they read.

Reflective questions

1. What is your vision for teaching reading? Consider what types of texts, tasks, and the context you envision to support aspects of your vision?

2. What about your students? If you are in the classroom, ask your students to share their vision of themselves as a learner. Encourage them to draw and write about it as well as outlining what their vision is for reading, writing, and in other subject areas. Talk with your students individually to help understand from their perspective what their vision is. If you are not in a classroom, what do you think a fifth grader or a third grader's vision for reading might be? Why these aspects?

3. Ask a colleague about their vision for teaching reading? See if you can see concrete practices that support these varying dimensions of their vision.

References

Allington, R. L. (2002). What I've learned about effective reading instruction: From a decade of studying exemplary elementary classroom teachers. *Phi Delta Kappan, 83*(10), 740–747.

Atwell, N. (2007). The pleasure principle. *Instructor, 116*(5), 44.

Bell, C. (2014). *El deafo*. Abrams.

Boushey, G., & Behne, A. (2019). *The CAFE book: Engaging all students in daily literacy assessment and instruction*. Stenhouse Publishers.

Boushey, G., & Moser, J. (2014). *The daily 5: Fostering literacy independence in the elementary grades*. Stenhouse Publishers.

Browne, A. (2014). *What if*. Candlewick.

Choi, Y. (2022). *The name jar*. Knopf Books for Young Readers.

Corno, L. (2004). Introduction to the special issue work habits and work styles: Volition in education. *Teachers College Record, 106*(9), 1669–1694.

Duffy, G. G. (2002). Visioning and the development of outstanding teachers. *Reading Research and Instruction, 41*(4), 331–344.

Gay, G. (2018). *Culturally responsive teaching: Theory, research, and practice*. Teachers College Press.

Hammerness, K. (2004). Teaching with vision: How one teacher negotiates the tension between high ideals and standardized testing. *Teacher Education Quarterly, 31*(4), 33–43.

Joy, A. (2020). *Black is a rainbow color*. Roaring Brook Press.

Moll, L. C., Amanti, C., Neff, D., & Gonzalez, N. (1992). Funds of knowledge for teaching: Using a qualitative approach to connect homes and classrooms. *Theory Into Practice, 31*(2), 132–141.

Muhammad, I. (2019). *The proudest blue: A story of hijab and family*. Little, Brown Books for Young Readers.

Pearson, P. D., & Gallagher, M. C. (1983). The instruction of reading comprehension. *Contemporary Educational Psychology, 8*(3), 317–344.

Pressley, M., Wharton-McDonald, R., Allington, R., Block, C. C., Morrow, L., Tracey, D., ... & Woo, D. (2001). A study of effective first-grade literacy instruction. *Scientific Studies of Reading, 5*(1), 35–58.

Pressley, M., Wharton-McDonald, R., Mistretta-Hampston, J., & Echevarria, M. (1998). Literacy instruction in 10 fourth-grade classrooms in upstate New York. *Scientific Studies of Reading, 2*(2), 159–194.

Singh, R. (2020). *111 trees: How one village celebrates the birth of every girl*. Kids Can Press.

Williams, V. B. (1982). *A chair for my mother*. Greenwillow Books.

· 4 ·

WHAT CAN A READER DO AND HOW CAN YOU USE ASSESSMENT TO GUIDE PRACTICE?

When Gradon came to work with Dixie, all she knew about him was that he was not meeting the end of year benchmarks outlined by the school for first grade. She had the scores from his practice tests and his year-end grades. But she needed more information about Gradon before she could offer him help. She started with some conversations about what he liked and what he didn't like. She asked him to read aloud and then she observed him reading to himself. She showed him a collection of books and asked him to pick one that he would like to be read to him. As she read, she paused for conversation about what he was thinking. It became clear that he had lots of thoughts but he did not recognize enough words to read the texts that he wanted to read. When he came to words he didn't know, he opted to guess quickly and move on to see if he could figure out the gist of the story.

Each component from test scores, conversations, and observations were critical to determining how to support Gradon. In this chapter we consider what a teacher can do by using an assessment framework: observations, conversations, and artifacts/testing. Additionally, we focus on how to use assessment information to design instruction.

Research on assessment

Over 25 years ago, Black and Wiliam (1998) observed that in spite of numerous district, state, and national initiatives and standards, the desired student learning outcomes and performances had not been achieved. Black and Wiliam argued that focusing on standards and test outcomes did not automatically translate to increased student performance. They suggested that assessment practices should include formative assessment. Formative assessment is "discovering what students know while they're still in the process of learning it" (Thomas, 2019, para. 1). It offers teachers the information they need to make necessary classroom and student level adjustments in the moment. It also provides students with important feedback during learning.

A deficit view of assessment focuses on finding what students cannot do. These deficits are often given labels such as "level 1" or "below proficiency." Students too often identify themselves with these labels, saying things like "I'm no good at reading." This can result in a cycle of viewing themselves as deficient (Johnston & Costello, 2005).

In contrast, a strengths-based view of assessment looks for what students can do. Strengths-based assessment also means that students should receive feedback about their results and progress and that such feedback should be helpful to them (Afflerbach & Cho, 2011). A strengths-based view of assessment recognizes that testing contexts are very specific and may not represent performances in other contexts (Baker, 2007; Johnston & Costello, 2005; Massey, 2020). What matters, then, is knowing our students and valuing them.

Assessment vs. testing

In this book, we distinguish between the terms "testing" and "assessment." Testing can be one component of assessment and is used to gather answers to specific questions such as "How many words does this student identify in a minute?" or "How many inferential questions can the student answer about this passage?" Assessment is about gathering information through multiple means. Assessment seeks to create a complex profile of a student by considering the student's background, strengths, and interests, and testing results with the purposes of providing a feedback loop for student growth and designing instruction (Black & Wiliam, 1998; Massey, 2020).

Our schools are full of data-driven instruction. Multiple data points are collected in the form of frequent progress monitoring. Neuman (2016) noted that data driven instruction is based on the following theoretical beliefs:

> Data collection can lead to more deliberate and systematic analysis of student work, which in turn can lead to more differentiated approaches to instruction that highlight individual students' strengths while working on their weaknesses, which can lead to greater student learning. This process is intended to create a carefully calibrated road map for instructional moves that will promote higher achievement. (p. 25)

Unfortunately, if we simply work from testing data, then all we know about the student is a "straight line" between the dates when we collect the testing data. As Neuman (2016) wrote, "Struggling readers know they're struggling readers. They do not need to see this confirmed every day" (p. 27). Additionally, because many schools have so many tests or data points that are required, teachers may feel like they have too much information.

If, however, we gather a range of information that includes observations, conversation, and artifacts/testing we know more about the student (represented by everthing in the triangle, illustrated in Figure 4.2) and we have used different types of data to learn different things about the student. In research terms, this is called triangulation. In other words, we want to know the pattern of information that emerges from multiple types of data rather than just testing data.

Throughout the chapters in this book, you will see the framework of observation, conversation, artifacts/testing applied to particular areas of literacy. Taken together, we call this assessment. The goal of all assessments is not just to gather information and create profiles. In other words, information is not the same thing as knowing what to do with it. Dr. Leaf, a neuroscientist, cautioned, "We've sacrificed the processing of knowledge for the gathering of data. We are, without realizing it, training ourselves to not process but immediately jump to a quick solution and reactive opinions" (Leaf, 2021, p. 66). Our task as teachers is to gather a range of information and then begin to form a thoughtful plan for instruction.

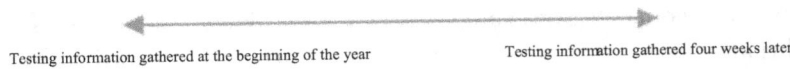

Testing information gathered at the beginning of the year   Testing information gathered four weeks later

Figure 4.1. Information from Testing

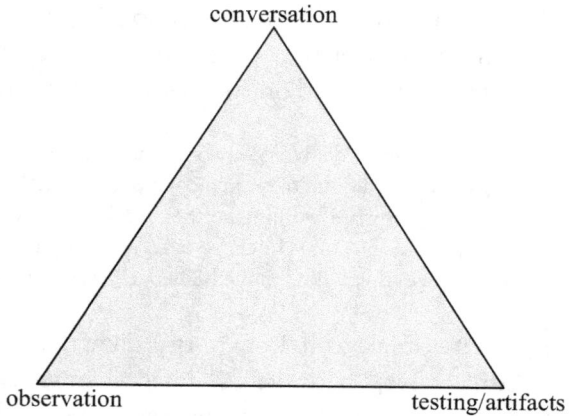

Figure 4.2. Assessment Framework

Information we need

Before we look at specifics about how we can implement the assessment framework, we need to know what we're assessing. Reading is often described as being composed of five pillars: phonemic awareness, phonics, fluency, vocabulary, and comprehension. one's ability to read is influenced by many factors beyond the five pillars. When it comes to assessment, we can categorize the pillars and outside factors into three separate areas: constrained skills, unconstrained skills, and other influences on skills.

Constrained skills: Phonemic awareness, phonics, and fluency

A constrained skill is a skill that has a limited number of concepts to acquire (Paris, 2005). Constrained skills in reading are phonemic awareness, phonics, and fluency. For example, learning the English alphabet requires identifying 26 discrete letters. Learning the number of sounds associated with those letters requires more concepts. Many count 44 phonemes in the English language and knowing these is considered to be constrained. Once the individual has learned the concepts, for example, they are considered to have mastered the skill (Paris, 2005).

Constrained skills are easier to test than unconstrained skills. For example, if you want to know if a student knows the letters in the alphabet, you can show her each letter—upper and lower case, and even different font types. You can test each of the concepts that make up alphabet knowledge. Because these skills are easier to test than unconstrained skills, these skills may be overemphasized to the exclusion of unconstrained skill instruction (Paris, 2005; Stahl, 2011). This happens in part, because teachers, the public, and policymakers "may equate success on constrained skills with reading proficiency (Paris, 2005, p. 201)." As a result, "minimum competency approach to reading assessment that does not adequately assess children's emerging use and control of literacy" (Paris, 2005, p. 201) may be created.

Unconstrained skills: Comprehension and vocabulary

An unconstrained skill is a meaning-based skill such as comprehension or vocabulary. These skills have a much longer developmental trajectory than constrained skills, meaning that they develop across a lifetime. One is never finished learning vocabulary or honing comprehension skills.

Additionally, an unconstrained skill is very individualistic. Think about watching a movie with a friend. One of you may frequently pause the movie or talk over the dialogue, asking questions and mentioning other connections or things the movie makes you think about. The other person may sit quietly, wanting to hear every word without interruption. Both of you may be actively making sense of the movie but you have very different approaches. The same is true for reading a text. One person may pause frequently to create a quick mental summary, write questions in the margins, underline words, and draw arrows to show how one line connects with another while another person reads the passage straight through and then rereads to make sure she understand. Both people may arrive at similar kinds of interpretations of the text but their process and the skills that they use differ. Individual processes may differ between genres or topics. That is, one person may use markedly different strategies when reading to comprehend a lease or loan agreement than when reading to comprehend a novel.

Unconstrained skills are more difficult to test. There is no simple level of mastery, making single measure inaccurate (Stahl, 2011). Quality assessment of unconstrained skills will require more time than assessment of constrained skills.

Other influences on skills

The list of possible influences on constrained and unconstrained skills is endless. In this book, we will talk about agency and motivation as areas that influence students' abilities to learn and use constrained and unconstrained skills.

Students' experiences outside of school play an important role in developing background knowledge and vocabulary knowledge that students bring to their reading. Students' languages, as well as their access and interest with books and language, all influence students' development of constrained and unconstrained skills.

Most teachers find out all they can about each student. There are questionnaires and surveys that ask about students' motivation, agency, likes and dislikes, and more. While we will talk about some in this book, our intent is not to identify specific tools. Instead, we hope to invite you to consider what other data sources would help you know the student and triangulate, or gather, a fuller picture of the student.

Applying the framework of assessment

What does implementation of the Framework of Assessment actually look like? In the following sections, we describe some ways to collect observation, conversation, and artifact/testing data. It is important to document data at the individual level, as well as to create a class profile that helps you look across students.

Observation

Observation first? This might seem like it goes against everything you've learned about teaching. Aren't you supposed to find out where your students are and build from there? Yes, but finding out where your students are does not depend on giving them a formal test. Even before you test, observe, and listen. We can learn a lot about our students simply by watching them. For example, if you work with emergent readers, you will find that some will eagerly pretend to read or view all of the pictures while others will immediately tell you that they can't read. That is an important distinction and gives you different openings to work with individual students.

An observation protocol can help guide your observations. The best protocols are ones that you design with your students and objectives in mind. Choose no more than three to five items to observe and plan to observe those same three to five elements across all students so that you can draw conclusions across students. It can also be helpful to designate a specific amount of time that you will observe individual students, such as five minutes. You will want to observe students regularly across time rather than observing randomly across the year.

Table 4.1. Observation Protocol

Names	When invited to read to self, does the student approach books, avoid books, or something in between? (Motivation to read)	When invited to read, how long can the student read/look at books before becoming distracted (stamina)	What genre does the student choose most often? Do they read the same series over and over or do they read multiple genres/types of books?	Do you notice anything about the sequence of reading—do they start at the front of the book and read straight through? Do they jump around?
1. Student 2. Student 3. 4. 5. ...				

At the beginning of the year, you might want to know more about their reading habits so that you can affirm their strengths and begin to offer targeted next steps. In Table 4.1, we offer an Observation Protocol but don't limit yourself to only the items in this example. Become learners about your students. Over the course of the year, the elements in the protocol will change.

Conversations and interviews

After you've had a chance to make some observations about each student, begin to talk to them about what you've observed as well as what they read. We've included some possible conversation starters that might accompany the observation protocol elements in the Observation Protocol (Table 4.1). Rather than going through one by one, try to choose one or two that you feel would help you understand something that you couldn't observe. Over time, you will add and delete topics of conversations. The goal is to learn more about students.

> ## Conversation Starters
>
> - What made you choose this book to read? Have you read it before? Have you read another in this series before?
> - What did you like about this book so far? Was there anything you didn't like about this book?
> - When you were reading yesterday, I noticed that you put several books back without reading. Can you tell me more about why you put the books back without reading them?
> - What books do you wish you could read? Why?
> - The last few times you've chosen books, I've noticed that you chose a _____ (series, genre, or author). Can you tell me more about why you choose those books?
> - What books do you wish we had in our classroom library? Why?

As teachers, we have to assume that we do not always understand why students are responding as they are. Consider one student we worked with who came in with his head down and often refused to interact in discussions about text. After multiple conversations and interactions with him, we discovered that his father was ill in the hospital. Now we saw his actions with a different lens! Many kids may not share their fears with us immediately, which is why we need to make space for ongoing and regular individual conversations, even if it's just a few minutes every few days.

It is important to have conversations with your students. We can also use more formal interviews and questionnaires about likes and dislikes connected to reading. There are many such interviews available online. We've also provided two interviews in Appendix A. One interview is intended for primary students, and one is intended for intermediate grades. The interviews focus on students' motivation to read, as well as their awareness of what it takes to be a good reader. Note that any of the interview questions could be given as a stand-alone question in a short conversation or to a small group of students.

Before we leave the topic of conversations and interviews, we want to mention that some of the most important things you will learn about a student will come from moments beyond the times that you plan to collect information. A student will tell you something on the way to the lunchroom or as you're lining students up to go home. We know of several teachers who carry a small notebook to lunch to record such things. We encourage you to see even these moments as data that can help you plan. These moments may offer you the insight that you need but you might not even recognize it in the rush of school. Elevate the importance of the small conversations through systematic collection.

Artifacts and testing

As a teacher, you will be asked to give lots of tests. Your district and/or curriculum will most likely dictate what tests you give and when you give them. These provide important information, but they are like taking a portrait photograph in a studio or formal area as opposed to taking a quick snapshot at the park. If you've ever been a part of wedding photographs, you know that the photographer works to get the lighting exactly right. You spend plenty of time standing around. Before long, your smile doesn't feel real, your feet might hurt, and you just want to be done. The photographs may be beautiful, but you know that you don't look like that most of the time.

Similarly, testing situations cause high anxiety for some students. Many tests are highly influenced by students' background experiences and the vocabulary that they already have prior to the test. It's helpful to keep in mind that students' scores might not be the same as what they could do in a less stressful situation. That's why we emphasize keeping artifacts as well as tests. Artifacts could be any work that exemplifies students' literacy skills. These include worksheets, journal entries, or other written artifacts. Artifacts could also include photographs of students working together during a book club discussion or an excerpt of a discussion that you heard between reading partners as they explained what they were thinking.

Just as with observations and conversations, even small things can add to the overall student profile. For example, a student wanted to add a sign to the classroom box of coins used for practicing with money. The student asked if she could write the word "bank" and put it on the box. The teacher gave her a sticky note and the student wrote "bak" for bank. The teacher copied this note and added it to her student artifacts to show the progress. In this instance, the b was formed correctly, showing growth for this student. The student included a vowel, demonstrating her emerging knowledge that words must have vowels. The student chose a k, perhaps demonstrating some familiarity with the word. This spelling aligned with what the student had done in a recent spelling profile where she omitted the preconsonantal nasals (the m in jump or the n in bank). In this way, the small note became a confirming piece of data that the student would benefit from some practice with word families that included preconsonantal nasals (e.g. -ink, -ank, -ump).

Managing the information

All of the information that you gather is only helpful if you can organize it into a useful manner. Most teachers find they must try a few different systems to find what works best for them. Some teachers keep a physical file for each student. As they write notes or collect artifacts, they simply file each new piece of information. Other teachers write electronic notes at regular intervals. Still other teachers keep a three-ring notebook with a section for each student. They carry sticky notes around with them and write down observations for a few focus students each day.

No matter the system, it is important to maintain a regular schedule for reviewing student work. Some teachers make space to sit down with the files of a few students (note that they don't try to keep up with every single student every day) and create a summary page (illustrated in Figure x.x) that is stapled to the front of the physical folder or saved to an electronic folder.

Data Collection Summary and Reflection

1. Summary of Observations from (date) to (date)
2. Summary of Conversations from (date) to (date)
3. Summary of Artifacts and Tests from (date) to (date)
4. Areas of strength
5. Areas showing student growth
6. Areas that need support and focused attention
7. Additional notes: (further questions, reminders for future data collection)

Just as we want to reflect on individual students, we also want to take time to reflect on our entire class. Some grade level teams reserve one or more of their meetings for this kind of data analysis. Working together can be very beneficial. Some teachers we know like to clear a wall or the floor and spread out the data so that they can physically look for patterns. Other teachers like spreadsheets. They enter testing data in some columns, student conversations in other columns, and observations in other columns. They can then use the search function to search for certain key phrases in their notes or sort columns with numerical values from highest to lowest. There is not one best system—only the system that works best for you.

We acknowledge that this takes time and time can be in short supply as a teacher. We can't give you more time, but we can offer a few suggestions from the teachers who are most consistent with this kind of data collection and reflection.

1. Focus on a few students per week. While you might collect testing data for all the students in your class on a single day, you will not be able to have meaningful conversations with every student in a day or even a week. We recommend that you start with students who are puzzling to you.
2. Find a system that works for you. If you hate spending more time on the computer, an electronic system probably isn't for you. If you hate all the individual pieces of paper, then a physical file is going to be hard for you to maintain.
3. Remind yourself that you are preparing for report cards and family conferences. While the time you spend reflecting on weekly data can seem like one more thing you don't have time to do, you will save yourself a lot of time when it comes to preparing report cards and conferencing with families. You will have a collection of information to reference.
4. Solicit student help. Students can learn to be part of the process. Many schools have student-led conferences. Students learn to collect their work and reflect on what they have learned. Invite them to be part of the process during the rest of the year. If they are old enough to write a sentence or more, they can add notes about what they've learned so far and why they think it's important. Self-reflection is a critical element of learning self-regulation.

We acknowledge the challenges of assessment using the assessment framework. Some of those are listed in Table 4.2. We encourage you to focus on what is best for individual students and what offers the most complete opportunities for knowing about the whole student.

Family involvement

Acknowledge and invite families into the process. Families are rich, diverse, and have a variety of experiences both positive and negative when it comes

Table 4.2. Challenges of Assessment in School

Challenges	Instructional Response
The district/school mandates which tests will be used.	Specify what information you will get from the test to identify what information is still needed. Triangulate data by adding observations and student interviews or conversations.
It is difficult to find time to add additional assessment data.	Begin small; focus on a small number of focal students who are.
The amount of information collected is overwhelming.	Create a system of organizing data to organize information and implement a regular time to reflect on the information collected.

to assessment. For example, one family member we know remembers struggling in school because of undiagnosed learning differences. He felt isolated in school. Now a parent, he wants to keep a close eye on all of his son's assessment results so that he can make sure he's not exhibiting any of the signs that his own teachers and family missed. Other families may feel unwelcome in school given traumatic experiences with schools. Recognize and honor this. Learn as much as you can about your students and their families. Families' approaches to schooling may come from a variety of emotions.

Finally, value the student above the student's scores. A teacher began the conference by reporting the results from a series of tests. The teacher then told the father how well the student was doing based on the test results. The father interrupted the teacher and asked, "Yes, but do you know my son?" This is an important reminder for all of us. We need to show caregivers that we want to know who their children are beyond assessments. Imagine how the father might have responded if the teacher started by asking him to share about his child and then began to share the many conversation notes she collected.

Focus on strengths, areas for further work, and what instruction you will be giving to support the student. Practice clear, concise communication about what matters when it comes to students' learning goals and the student's progress. Teach families how to read with their children and talk about books. Make sure they have materials at home to read. Be sure to invite families to tell you more about the student and what they observe at home.

Reflective questions

1. What are some assessment practices you've seen in schools? What worked to help provide a full portrait of students? What didn't?

2. Reflect on a time when you were involved in some type of high-stakes assessment. What was helpful/unhelpful about the assessment? Did you receive any feedback? How was the feedback helpful/unhelpful?

3. What are some high-stakes educational issues affecting you locally? Are there assessments connected to this and if so, what role do they play?

References

Afflerbach, P. P., & Cho, B. Y. (2011). The classroom assessment of reading. In M. Kamil, P. D. Pearson, E. Moje, & P. Afflerbach (Eds.), *Handbook of reading research-IV* (pp. 487–514). Routledge.
Baker, E. L. (2007). 2007 presidential address—The end (s) of testing. *Educational Researcher*, 36(6), 309–317.
Black, P., & Wiliam, D. (1998). *Inside the black box: Raising standards through classroom assessment*. Granada Learning.
Johnston, P., & Costello, P. (2005). Principles for literacy assessment. *Reading Research Quarterly*, 40(2), 256–267.
Leaf, C. (2021). *Cleaning up your mental mess*. Baker Books.
Massey, D. D. (2020). Assessment practices in literacy. In S. Parsons & M. Vaughn (Eds.), *Best practices in literacy*. Guilford Press.
Neuman, S. B. (2016). Code red: The danger of data-driven instruction. *Educational Leadership*, 74(3), 24–29.
Paris, S. G. (2005). Reinterpreting the development of reading skills. *Reading Research Quarterly*, 40(2), 184–202.
Stahl, K. (2011). Applying new visions of reading development in today's classroom. *The Reading Teacher*, 65(1), 52–56.
Thomas., L. (2019). Seven smart, fast ways to do formative assessment. *Edutopia Weekly*. Retrieved from https://www.edutopia.org/article/7-smart-fast-ways-do-formative-assessment/

Part II
Dispositional

· 5 ·

HOW CAN YOU FOSTER READING MOTIVATION?

Tori was an avid reader through the fifth grade—disappearing for hours and hours to read all of the Harry Potter series, Kwame Alexander's books, and the latest graphic novel series. Suddenly, she quit, she quit. She didn't want books as presents. She didn't want to go to the library or buy books. What happened? She seemingly was unmotivated to read. Interestingly, Tori's story is not unique. We've heard similar stories from frustrated teachers and distraught parents. But what can we do to change things? Understanding motivation is critical when teaching reading and working to support any reading difficulties students may experience when it comes to reading.

Research on motivation

What exactly is motivation? Motivation is a construct "used to explain the initiation, direction, intensity, and persistence of behavior, especially goal-directed behavior" (Brophy, 1983, p. 3). Motivation includes whether or not students feel as though they have the ability to accomplish a task. If students have the self-efficacy or the belief that they can succeed they will pursue a task. If they believe they do not have the skills necessary, they will more than likely avoid pursuing a task (Wigfield, 1994). Students are not "motivated" or "unmotivated" to read. Their motivation exists all along a continuum between approaching or avoiding reading (see Figure 5.1).

Approaching or avoiding reading is influenced by several key factors:

- *Expectancy*: Does the student *expect* to be able to complete the task—reading the text with understanding? If there are other tasks that have been added to the reading such as taking a test about the reading, participating in a discussion, or writing a paragraph, what is the student's expectancy for those additional tasks? It is possible that the student expects to be able to do the reading but does not expect to do well on the additional task. In that case, the motivation for the reading itself is fine but the motivation for the additional task is low and may result in the student trying to avoid the additional tasks by ignoring the assignment, disrupting the environment, or employing other avoidance strategies.
- *Value*: Does the student *value* the reading? If students to not value the text because the topic seems irrelevant to them, they may seek to avoid the reading. As with expectancy, it may be the associated task. In other words, the student may value the reading while not valuing the school-assigned task. We have heard many students tell us that the book they were reading was fine, but they hated completing the double-entry notes, sticky note annotations, or worksheets. This is frequently accompanied by the question, "Why can't I just read the book?"
- *Ability*: Do they have the *ability* to decode, hold the word meanings in their short term memory, and think about meaning? We draw a distinction between students who are learning to decode and do not like to

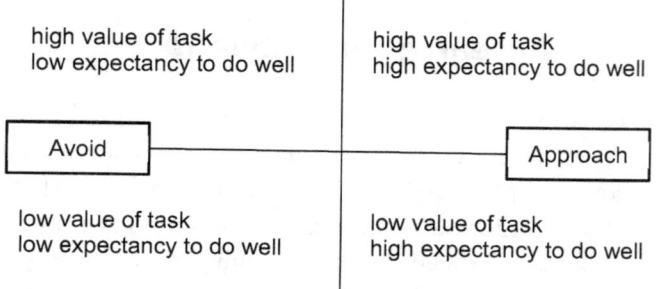

Figure 5.1. Expectancy-Value Continuum of Motivation

read or the process of learning to crack the code (covered in Chapter 7) and students who have learned to decode and can decode fluently with understanding and yet choose not to read.
- *Community Participation*: Motivation also has a social component. Students may be willing to approach things they would not otherwise approach if it is important to their community of acceptance. However, if the task does not elevate their social connectedness within their desired communities of acceptance, they will often choose to avoid the task rather than risk being in discord with their communities. Consider students who place a high value on reading by visiting the library and talking about the books they have read with family, friends, and others. If students value that community, they may read more so as to have something to contribute to that community. However, over time, students may become part of another friend group that values gaming over reading and encourages spending more time online. Choosing to read instead of engaging in the games risks creating dissonance with friends.

It is important to understand the theory of expectancy-value of motivation when it comes to reading because if students lack the confidence and the skills to approach a reading task, more than likely they will avoid taking on such a text. Students may disengage in what they are reading. They may also exhibit unwanted behaviors such as the challenges summarized in Table 5.1.

Table 5.1. Challenges to Motivation in Reading in School

Challenge	Instructional Response
Students only want to read the same book/series	Encourage students to talk to one another about books.
Pick up the books and then abandon them	Interview students about why they are abandoning the books Ask them if they had someone to read with them as a partner would they continue? Focus on building reading stamina a few minutes at a time. Don't require that students continue to read a book they are no longer interested in- there are too many good books to read!
They resist reading and the tasks associated with reading	Interview students to understand their resistance, ask students how they could show you that they understand the text or the task in a different way. Don't force students to complete a series of tasks with a book they dislike.

Instruction that supports motivation

In order to be effective, instruction requires two components—a systematic plan implemented with consistency. A systematic plan avoids the random nature of a collection of activities. Systematic plans ensure that the tasks get more complex and move in the direction of greater student autonomy.

Even the best plans fail if not implemented consistently over time. Anyone who has started an exercise program can verify that large amounts of exercise spread out randomly across time will result in sore muscles or even injury and very few gains. Similarly, when implementing a plan to support student motivation, the timing of implementation is as important as the content of the plan. Before you begin, be purposeful about when and how often you can include the plan's components in your instructional routines. It is better to implement the plan for 15 minutes twice a week as opposed to 30 minutes once a week, but even once a week on a weekly basis is preferable to inclusion at random intervals.

We have organized our plan with the title: ABCDEs of Instruction to Encourage Motivation (Table 5.2).

Assess

As described in Chapter 4 on Assessment, the assessment framework includes observations, conversations, and artifacts/testing. While we recommend beginning with observation, in reality, you will need to adapt the order of these

Table 5.2. ABCDEs of Instruction to Encourage Motivation

ABCDEs of Instruction to Encourage Motivation	
Assess	Observation, conversation, and artifacts/testing are used to create a classroom profile of motivation across the year.
Balance student choice and teacher voice	Provide some choice of texts and tasks for students.
Cultivate curiosity	Create environments where students can be curious and develop interests. Allow students to ask questions.
Demonstrate social skills	Provide opportunities for students to demonstrate their knowledge and learning with peers.
Evaluation	Help students evaluate their own learning and set goals for new learning.

components to your classroom. Over time, you will come to see every interaction with a student as some type of information that adds to their overall profile. Specific to motivation, the framework will include the following elements:

Observations

Observations should play a crucial part in any assessment. Teachers notice and wonder things about their students constantly. The key is to record these noticing and wonderings in a systematic way across time. For example, choose two are three focal students during independent reading time or small group time. During their reading or soon after, spend a few minutes making notes about each student. Observe what they do when they pick a book or when they're reading a book by beginning with the question, "Are they approaching or avoiding reading?"

Do not be discouraged that you don't get to every student every week. If you get to each student just one time a month, you will still have nine specific observations focused on their motivation. These observations give additional information for conversations with students, for purposes of grouping, and for sharing with families. You may find that you want to do additional observations with students that are particularly puzzling to you.

Data points

Good instruction begins with knowing something about your students. Many teachers begin the year with interest surveys. These are a great start but there is so much else to learn beyond students' interests. Fortunately, we have many free online questionnaires that have been designed to help us learn more about students' motivation. Here are a few surveys that are public domain:

Elementary reading attitude survey (McKenna & Kear, 1990)

In this survey for first through sixth graders, students are presented with a Likert-type scale of Garfield, the cartoon character. Garfield's expression ranges from happy to unhappy in four separate choices. Students circle the expression closest to how they feel about reading and writing. The survey may be given to a whole class. Scores can be organized around recreational reading (or writing), academic reading (or writing) and total scores.

Motivation to read profile-revised (Malloy, Marinak, Gambrell, & Mazzoni, 2013)

This survey is designed for upper elementary and middle school students. It can be administered to the whole class to determine students' self-perception of the value of reading and themselves as readers.

Interviews

Surveys and observations give you important information about your students' motivation. It is also helpful to talk to students and their families. One way to begin is by conferencing with individual students after you have conducted an observation. Ask them about any questions that were raised from the observation and record their answers with your observation notes. When you meet with families during conferences, share your observations with the families and ask them to describe what they see at home about their student's motivation. For example, you might ask the families to describe a time when their student has been very motivated to complete any task, not necessarily reading. Then ask them to describe a time when their student avoids a task. After starting at the general level, repeat both questions about reading and/or writing specifically.

One of our favorite interview questions is inspired by Csikszentmihalyi's (1990) description of flow, or that complete focus and immersion when you are in the zone. Csikszentmihalyi noted that flow tends to occur in specific situations where there are clear goals or when there is a challenge that is almost too difficult but still accomplishable. To better understand if students have ever experienced a moment of flow connected to learning, we ask students if they've ever been so interested in something they've been doing that they've lost track of time. Sometimes we give examples from students we've taught previously. For example, one student said he lost track of time when he was cooking with his grandmother. One told us she lost track of time when she was playing Minecraft with her friend. Based on their responses, we follow up by asking if they've ever had the experience of losing track of time in school. Their responses are great information to record as part of each student's individual observation. We let students know that our goal is to create many environments where flow can happen for them.

After initial assessment, there are two additional steps that are critical. First, use the information gathered to create a classroom profile. If using something like the *Motivation to Read* (Malloy et al., 2013) profile, a classroom profile can show you how many students have a low value of reading vs. students who have a higher value of reading. This will aid you in grouping students across the profiles. Second, be sure to continue to assess throughout the year. School age students change rapidly. What interested them last month may no longer interest them this week. Their motivation to read may shift from day to day with no warning. This is normal and part of their development. Celebrate changes but don't hold them to being motivated by the same things for too long.

Balance student choice and teacher voice

The research is remarkably strong in support of this idea. If we want to create environments where students demonstrate sustained motivation, they must have choices in two areas: choice in texts they read and choice in tasks they complete. The "balancing" element of this choice recognizes that the teacher (and the curriculum) will require students to complete texts and tasks, but for sustained motivation, students must also have authentic choices.

Text choices

One way to provide student text choices is to set aside time for independent reading. This is prefaced upon having regular time to read and having a robust classroom library where students have ample choices and time to choose. Consider setting aside a minimum of 10 minutes for primary grades and a minimum of 15 minutes for intermediate grades and increase this time incrementally throughout the year.

Regular time is critical. If the time happens only occasionally, students will not be able to track the story. Think of a time when you tried to read a long book or watch a movie and you had constant interruptions, or you had to come back several days later. Chances are, it took some time to remind yourself what was going on. You might have decided to start over or abandon it all together. Schools are complex places with numerous distractions and interruptions. By providing regular time to read a text of choice, you create opportunities for engagement.

Some children will choose the same book or series over and over again. Rather than express concern, this is a time when they should be allowed to choose those familiar texts. Consider letting them form "fan groups" where they can talk about these favorite books with others. Encourage students to recommend these books to others in the class and wider school community.

Even providing a choice of texts for students who struggle to value reading or do not consider themselves readers will not be enough for some students to sustain motivation for reading. We recommend not requiring students to do more than track what books they've tried. Requiring annotations, a certain number of pages, or book reviews will shift the focus to the task and not the enjoyment of reading for those students who struggle to be motivated to read.

Tasks

Students should also be given some choice about the tasks associated with reading. These choices can be small, such as choices of reading an assigned story independently, with a partner, or joining you for a small group meeting. Choices can be much broader, as well. After allowing students to choose a topic of interest, Massey and Miller (2022) asked students to be able to show the class what they learned in a 10–15 minute presentation. Some students created powerpoints. Some created posters. Some set up interviews. Be responsive and adaptive in your approach.

Cultivate curiosity

Students come to school with particular interests, but these are limited by what they have experienced. Cultivating curiosity is about introducing them to new ideas and experiences. The first step of cultivating curiosity is generating interest. Interest is frequently easy to generate. An unusual picture displayed on the screen. A puzzling question. An experiment. A cliff-hanging chapter.

Interest may quickly dissipate when they are asked to read more, answer questions, or get into discussion groups. This flash of interest has been referred to as situational interest. While sustained interest is much harder to support, it begins with situational interest. How do you create this initial situational interest?

The first step is to create an environment where students are invited to be curious by modeling your own interest and curiosity. Offer short comments such as that might begin with, "Do you know what I read last night?" You can present a question or a puzzle and invite interest. You might present a portion of text and ask, "What do you think this is about and why?" You might bring in a science experiment and ask students what they think will happen. You might present an artifact connected to a social studies unit and ask students what they think it was used for and why. Key to each of these questions is not just answering the initial question but giving students additional sources to explore. For example, when studying state history, one teacher used the items from the local museum available for classroom use. She displayed the items and asked students to imagine who used each item and for what purpose. Students had two days to consider. After that, the teacher had a table of photos, single paragraphs, and in some cases longer texts where students could find the artifacts and identify the use. As teachers, it's easy to get excited and tell students the answers, especially when we've kept them in suspense. However, to truly support situational interest it is better to give students the opportunities to find the answers.

At other times, you will invite students to ask the questions and search together to find answers. Daniels (2017) offers a wonderful description of this in his book, *The Curious Classroom*. He worked with a group of teachers to develop interests, including:

- Setting up a wonder wall with students' questions—and answers
- Beginning each day with "soft-starts" where students are allowed to have 10–15 minutes at the beginning of each school day for things like purposeful play, meeting with classroom buddies, or pursue a mini-inquiry
- Following the news, including local, national, and state news, or an appropriate webcam
- Spending time with experts by inviting local professionals to the classroom, hosting a virtual visit, or sending emails with questions

Sometimes the interest in these soft starts ended quickly. At other times, students discovered a passion that they didn't know they had and spent significant time on it over the course of the school year.

We offer one caution about generating interest. As teachers, we need to give up the notion that if we are creative enough, we can make a lesson interesting or find books that will interest students, all of the time. Have you ever watched young children at the park? Two children may be happily playing on the climbing bars. If two other children walk into the park and begin to play at the sandbox, the two on the swings may quickly lose interest in the swings and drift to the sandbox. Does it mean they are no longer interested in the swings? Not necessarily. They may simply be more curious about the newcomers. Insisting that they stay interested in the swings will take either a lot of adult coaxing and attention or result in upset children.

Demonstrate social competence

Decades of research has emphasized how important being able to demonstrate competency to others is for student motivation. This can look differently for different students. Some students will play it safe and stick with topics or texts that are familiar. This is sometimes a risk-avoiding strategy. They don't want to fail or be viewed as dumb so they will avoid (instead of approach) topics, texts, and tasks that seem unfamiliar and might result in being viewed as less than knowledgeable or competent.

When planning ways for students to demonstrate social competence, consider the following:

- Consider audience. If students are asked to read and respond to questions that only the teacher reads, they are not demonstrating social competence. However, encouraging them to share their knowledge with others may foster social competence.
- Provide some opportunities for students to choose who they present to and how they present. For example, when discussing a text, some students might choose to talk with one other person and some might choose to talk in a larger group. Both can happen at the same time in a classroom.
- Offer open-ended tasks that allow multiple and varied responses. For example, students might write about why they think a character responded in a particular way. Providing evidence supports many of the literacy standards, but a range of options are possible.
- Create community through literature circles, book clubs, and reader's theater performing groups. The goals for these groups include supporting comprehension, demonstrating social competence, as well speaking and listening goals. Model how to respond to others with the use of sentence stems, affirmative statements, and friendly suggestions.

Evaluation

Evaluation that supports motivation encourages personal evaluation rather than outside evaluation. This kind of evaluation asks students to consider how they did personally. It asks them to be reflective about their learning of the content and their participation as a member of the group. A final important component is goal setting for future work. Consider the example evaluation from a book club. Over time, students can offer suggestions for changes or create their own evaluation.

> **Book Club Self-Evaluation**
>
> - What did you learn from this book?
> - Did I offer affirmations to the group? What were they?
> - Did I offer friendly suggestions? What were they?
> - Do you think this group worked well together? Why?
> - How could you help your group work better together?
> - What goal or goals do you have for the next book we read in class?
> - What goal or goals do you have for working with others in class?

Some students used to love reading; now they don't? What happened?

Students worldwide are reading less and choose to read for fun less than ever before (National Literacy Trust, 2022; Schaeffer, 2021). The intermediate grades are a time of transition in many areas, including reading. Chall (1983) noted the transition from learning to read to reading to learn. In younger grades, students are learning how to read. Instruction is focused on building necessary skills such as alphabet knowledge, decoding, and fluency. The types of texts students encounter are focused on supporting these skills. When students crack the code of reading and are reading fluently, instruction shifts toward a focus on comprehension and deeper understanding. This typically happens in the intermediate grades (fourth and up) where students read more complex texts focused on domain specific content. Texts are known to be increasingly more complex and students are reading to learn about specific content.

Unfortunately, there is a long history of research describing the challenges of readers in the intermediate grades. The challenge, termed as the fourth grade slump, identifies a phenomenon where students' reading scores may decline (Brozo, 2005; Chall & Jacobs, 2003) as they transition between learning to read and reading to learn. No single factor explains this decline in students' scores, but some contributing factors may include the following:

- Lack of fluency and automaticity in recognition of words and phrases, resulting in reading less and avoiding difficult materials (Chall, 1983; Chall & Jacobs, 2003).

- Decelerating vocabulary learning of less common words, affecting overall comprehension (Chall & Jacobs, 2003)
- Increasing textual demands, specifically in expository texts (Best, Floyd, & McNamara, 2004).
- Lack of world knowledge required to understand expository texts and new concepts and make inferential conclusions about text (Best, Floyd, & McNamara, 2004).
- Increasing number of distractions students encounter, including electronic media (Svensen, 1999).
- Curricular constraints that result in reading tasks that are unrelated to students' goals and/or interests (Gallagher, 2009).
- Shifting communities of acceptance (Li & Stone, 2018) which means that students' peer groups change and they face a myriad of social challenges.

Of course, it's not only fourth graders who are affected. Students not just in the United States but worldwide are reading less and choose to read for fun less than ever before (National Literacy Trust, 2022; Schaeffer, 2021). This decline was evident when reading physical books and when listening to audio books (National Literacy Trust, 2022). While recent surveys of reading enjoyment are certainly influenced by the pandemic, the trend downward has been occurring for decades.

At this point, the outlook may feel bleak. However, research also offers a more hopeful picture. Consider a few studies of deep student interest:

- Johnston et al. (2020) described work with students in kindergarten through third grade who were allowed to write books about their own lives and about topics they were interested in at the beginning of the school year. Throughout the year, they continued to write books, engage in deep conversation around texts, and build knowledge together. Not only did they meet their goals for conversation and engagement, but the students were also reading increasingly more difficult texts.
- Miller et al. (2022) described a fourth grade classroom where the teacher noted students' lack of understanding about a curriculum-prescribed passage on bacteria. Instead of moving on with the prescribed pace of the curriculum, the teacher extended the topic with additional experiments. Ultimately, the teacher suspended the curriculum for a few weeks to follow students' interests. Students read widely, conducted experiments,

and helped shape what they studied next. When compared with other fourth grade students in the school, this teacher's students scored higher on end of grade assessments even though they had not covered all of the prescribed curriculum.
- Massey and Miller (2022) worked with middle school readers who were identified as struggling readers by their school for academic or motivational reasons. The primary focus of instruction was allowing students to choose a topic of interest, read within the topic, and ultimately share what they learned with their peers through a final presentation. Students reported being more motivated to learn in this way, working harder than they normally would in school, and reading more than normal.

What does this all mean? Regardless of age, students who are interested are more motivated to read and learn, they demonstrate higher-level cognitive strategies, and are more persistent through learning challenges (Ainley et al., 2002; Lin-Siegler et al., 2016).

So why don't we see more instruction that is formed by students' interests? Miller et al. (2022) wrote:

> The simplicity of this recommendation runs counter to the realities of classroom life where teachers are expected to follow pacing guides that focus on designated topics with limited time allocated to studying any one of them. -- if students provide the lead for instruction, will teachers follow? Educators of different persuasions commonly emphasize the importance of beginning instruction based on students' present levels (Ausubel, 2012; Hattie, 2009; Nelson et al., 2015). Unfortunately, such recommendations fail to consider students' interests as a primary starting point. Instead, reforms usually focus on increasing interest within an established curriculum, not on using students' ideas and concerns as an actual starting point for designing instruction. (Pintrich, 2003, p. 52)

In other words, we know a lot about how to support students' desires to read: give them time to read, time to explore topics and/or books opportunities to talk with others, and opportunities to share with others in meaningful-to-them ways (Brandt et al., 2021).

In spite of the invitations and supports we provide; some students will not be motivated to read everything we offer. We experienced this as teachers and as parents. Tori, described in the opening of this chapter, is Dixie's daughter. It is not an exaggeration to say that Dixie panicked. Because so much of Dixie's identity was and is as a reader and as a teacher of reading, the self-doubt was immediate. Dixie knew she must have done something "wrong."

By the time Tori reached her sophomore year of high school, she began edging back into reading—none of the books that Dixie suggested, but that wasn't the point. When she asked to go to a bookstore, Dixie silently rejoiced. No single thing made the difference, but a few things were clear:

- Students will try out many different identities. If they have been a reader, they may try out being the opposite—a non-reader.
- Provide access. Buy books and leave them lying around. Invite them to a bookstore or library.
- Don't pressure the student to read. Invite them to read without criticism.
- Continue to talk about your own reading.
- Build interests with experiences they enjoy. Ultimately, the relationship that you build will be even more important than what they read so emphasize the relationship over reading time.

Reflective questions

1. Consider your classroom library. What books do students read most often? Check with your school librarian. What books are most frequently asked for or checked out? What "look-alike" books could you add to your library that are like the popular books and might offer a next read for your students?

2. When have you observed students experiencing high motivation in school? List the texts, tasks, and social dynamics of the setting. Share your observations with students and ask them to give you feedback about their experiences.

3. Look at your literacy block plans for a single week. What adaptations could you make that would allow students to have more choices?

References

Ainley, M., Hillman, K., & Hidi, S. (2002). Gender and interest processes in response to literary texts: Situational and individual interest. *Learning and Instruction, 2*(4), 411–428.
Ausubel, D. P. (2012). *The acquisition and retention of knowledge: A cognitive view.* Kluwer Academic Publishers.

Best, R., Floyd, R. G., & McNamara, D. S. (2004, April). Understanding the fourth-grade slump: Comprehension difficulties as a function of reader aptitudes and text genre. In *85th Annual Meeting of the American Educational Research Association*.

Brandt, L., Sharp, A. C., & Gardner, D. S. (2021). Examination of teacher practices on student motivation for reading. *The Reading Teacher*, 74(6), 723–731.

Brophy, J. (1983). Conceptualizing student motivation. *Educational Psychologist*, 18(3), 200–215.

Brozo, W. G. (2005). Avoiding the "fourth-grade slump". *Thinking Classroom*, 6(4), 48.

Chall, J. S. (1983). *Stages of reading development*. McGraw-Hill.

Chall, J. S., & Jacobs, V. A. (2003). Poor children's fourth-grade slump. *American Educator*, 27(1), 14–17.

Csikszentmihalyi, M. (1990). Literacy and intrinsic motivation. *Daedalus*, 115–140.

Daniels, H. (2017). *The curious classroom*. Heinemann.

Gallagher, K. (2009). *Readicide: How schools are killing reading and what you can do about it*. Stenhouse.

Hattie, J. (2009). The black box of tertiary assessment: An impending revolution. *Tertiary Assessment & Higher Education Student Outcomes: Policy, Practice & Research*, 259, 275.

Johnston, P. H., Champeau, K., Helmer, S., Hartwig, A., Komar, M., McCarthy, L., & Krueger, T. (2020). *Engaging literate minds: Developing children's social, emotional, and intellectual lives, K-3*. Stenhouse Publishers.

Li, M., & Stone, H. N. (2018). A social network analysis of the impact of a teacher and student community on academic motivation in a science classroom. *Societies*, 8(3), 68.

Lin-Siegler, X., Dweck, C. S., & Cohen, G. L. (2016). Instructional interventions that motivate classroom learning. *Journal of Educational Psychology*, 108(3), 295.

Malloy, J. A., Marinak, B. A., Gambrell, L. B., & Mazzoni, S. A. (2013). Assessing motivation to read: The motivation to read profile–revised. *The Reading Teacher*, 67(4), 273–282.

Massey, D. D., & Miller, S. D. (2022). What comes first? The Zombies or the skills?. *Voices From the Middle*, 30(2), 27–30.

McKenna, M. C., & Kear, D. J. (1990). Measuring attitude toward reading: A new tool for teachers. *The Reading Teacher*, 43(9), 626–639.

Miller, S., Stallings, S., Massey, D., & Metzger, S. R. (2022). A lesson in motion stays in motion: If students lead, will teachers follow?. *Phi Delta Kappan*, 104(4), 48–53.

National Literacy Trust. (2022). Children and young people's listening in 2022. Retrieved from https://literacytrust.org.uk/research-services/research-reports/children-and-young-peoples-listening-in-2022

Nelson, P. M., Ysseldyke, J. E., & Christ, T. J. (2015). Student perceptions of the classroom environment: Actionable feedback to guide core instruction. *Assessment for Effective Instruction*, 41(1), 16–27.

Pintrich, P. R. (2003). A motivational science perspective on the role of student motivation in learning and teaching contexts. *Journal of Educational Psychology*, 95(4), 667.

Schaeffer. (2021). Among many U.S. children, reading for fun has become less common, federal data shows. Pew Research Center. Retrieved from https://www.pewresearch.org/short-reads/2021/11/12/among-many-u-s-children-reading-for-fun-has-become-less-common-federal-data-shows/

Svensen, A. (1999). When kids hate to read. *Reading Rockets*. Retrieved from https://www.readingrockets.org/article/when-kids-hate-read

Wigfield, A. (1994). Expectancy-value theory of achievement motivation: A developmental perspective. *Educational Psychology Review, 6,* 49–78.

· 6 ·

HOW CAN YOU SUPPORT AGENTIC READERS?

The other day when Margaret visited middle schoolers and asked them to describe what they enjoyed about their language arts class, many of the students said, "We finally get to choose what we want to read." In other words, these students experienced a sense of agency in their work as readers. The role of agency is perhaps one of the most vital aspects of supporting readers. But what exactly is student agency? Student agency is defined as, "a student's ability to have ideas, intentions, and to exert influence and take actions to expand the learning context" (Vaughn, 2020a, p. 115). When you hear this definition, it may remind you of providing opportunities during reading instruction where students are in charge of their learning, involved in projects and activities that are meaningful to them, and encouraged to pursue learning interests both individually and collectively.

We are often approached by teachers about why many of their students seem disinterested in reading. Notable literacy researcher, Linda Gambrell, states, "I have been convinced that the central and most important goal of reading instruction is to foster a love of reading" (1996, p. 5). As we discussed in Chapters 3, creating equitable instructional spaces is paramount. The ways in which classroom materials are shared and how reading instruction is organized to motivate students is vital when structuring reading opportunities.

Perhaps though, a less well known component of cultivating a love of reading is what scholars have termed, "student agency."

Research on student agency

For the last several years, we have studied student agency in a variety of classrooms and in our own teaching (Miller et al., 2022; Vaughn, 2013, 2014, 2016, 2018, 2020a, b, 2021; Vaughn & Massey, 2021). Effective reading teachers foster student agency in their classrooms. We have seen powerful ways in which student agency is taken up and what it means for students but have also seen where agency seems to have been denied to students. What exactly does student agency look like in practice? Consider the following example. During a summer writing workshop, sixth graders led their peers in the creation of a multimodal book trailer. The lesson was focused on having students create a written piece based on a genre of interest. Another aspect of the lesson included encouraging students to use materials flexibly and at their own pace. Two students, skilled in using a variety of applications, decided to turn their book trailer into an animated series. These students taught others in the class how to use the animation app and the strategies they used to incorporate specific details about the texts they read into their creation.

During this experience, students were in charge of their learning, they had flexibility in the ways in which they pursued their interests and worked individually and collectively to accomplish their goal. Simultaneously, a core component of the instruction was focusing on how to foster a love of reading. In fact, motivation is one dimension of agency. In the classroom, books of all levels and genres were displayed, much like in a bookstore, and students shopped daily for books they wanted to and were motivated to read. All genres were encouraged by the teacher. During the reading segment, students read for close to 30 minutes on their own and often wanted to keep reading even when the class had ended for the day. How was student agency supported in this classroom?

- Students had flexibility in how they shared and pursued what they wanted to create and read.
- The classroom environment encouraged students to engage in a variety of meaningful activities, central to their interests.
- Students' ideas were taken seriously and as a result, students participated in the learning process and were co-collaborators.

Dimensions of student agency

In the above example, you may ask, "Isn't supporting agency like this just good teaching?" Yes! Effective and equitable teaching supports students' agency, specifically three dimensions of agency (Vaughn, 2018) that we outline next:

1. Dispositional: This references students' inner dispositions, their ideas, intentions, and what it is they want to accomplish as a result of their learning.
2. Motivational: Along the motivational dimension of agency, students' are involved in activities during reading instruction where they are supported to pursue tasks that are interesting and relevant to their lives.
3. Positional: The positional dimension of agency outlines how students are positioned in the classroom. In other words, are students being supported in their learning pursuits? Along this dimension, teachers must ask themselves about how students are viewed in the classroom. Are they active contributors?

What do these dimensions look like in practice?

Dispositional

In order to support reading instruction along the dispositional dimension, teachers can do the following:

- Provide student choice in what they are reading.
- Invite students to share about what they are reading with others.
- Encourage project based learning and involving students in reading for authentic purposes, where students can decide and pursue topics of interest.

One of the ways we see students' dispositions encouraged during reading instruction is to have students keep a Reading Notebook where they document important books they've read as well as deciding which books they want to read while providing feedback on books read.

In these Reading Notebooks (See Image 6.1), students are encouraged to respond to what they are reading in a variety of modes that they choose from written to visual as well as by writing in a variety of genres from poetry to fiction. As seen in this example, the student responds to the story, *Ender's Becoming* (Card, 2021) and makes critical inferences about the plot.

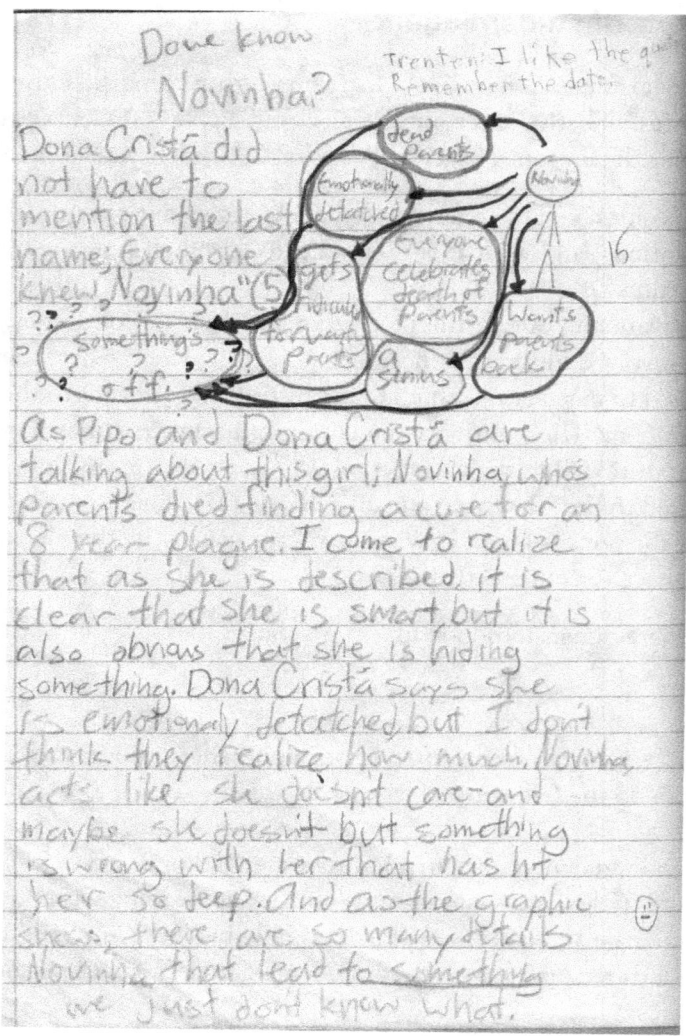

Image 6.1. Seventh Grade Reading Notebook

Motivational

By providing choice in how students pursue knowledge learned, this connects with the motivational dimension aspect of agency. Along this dimension of agency, teachers can think strategically about the types of tasks and activities they require of students. For example, teachers can structure opportunities where students have a voice and say in what they are reading and how they want to share knowledge learned. This can be structured in a variety of ways. Some ideas include: a checklist where students can choose the type of activity they want to create after finishing a book, or flexible grouping where students are encouraged to work collaboratively with one another or independently. Instructional opportunities are focused on students' interests and motivations.

Positional

When it comes to the positional dimension of agency, teachers can invite students into the curriculum by asking students what it is they want to learn and how they want to learn. A concrete practice teachers can do is to invite students to share their reading visions. These visions serve to ask students what it is they wish to accomplish with their reading and how they plan to work toward achieving these reading goals.

In this first grader's vision, he shared that he "would like to have 30 minutes to read and pick any book that's appropriate." When asked how and why this was his vision he shared, "Well, I want to build up the time to be able to read on my own for 30 minutes and then pick out a book that's not too scary or has anything really scary in it. I don't like reading about scary stuff." By eliciting visions like this and asking students to share what it is they want to accomplish, we can find ways to support students in their reading goals.

Image 6.2. First Grade Reading Vision

Challenges with agency

There are several barriers when it comes to supporting student agency during reading instruction. We've organized them into two different categories where we briefly discuss them below:

External: These barriers include factors often outside of teacher control. This includes district-wide or school mandates that prescribe literacy curricula that teachers must use when teaching reading. Although many of these programs have positive features, the prescriptive nature of such programs rarely aligns with providing individualized and specialized instruction to students. Moreover, given the prescriptive nature, there are minimal opportunities where students have choice and voice in what they are doing. As a result, external barriers, as well as a lack of resources to implement flexible instructional opportunities (i.e., minimal variety of texts and genres), can result in minimal opportunities for student agency.

Internal: Internal barriers include the tension of supporting student agency and maintaining the balance between targeting instructional skills while also providing opportunities for student-led instruction. Recently, we interviewed students about whether they felt they had ideas that should be included in their classroom. Overwhelmingly, students shared that they felt as though the teacher was the one that should be telling them about what to learn and that they should not provide the class with direction during reading instruction. Of course, teachers are skilled professionals and should direct the learning as they have knowledge of reading pedagogies, however, students also have insight and knowledge that is critical. We encourage asking students about what it is they want to do as well as their views about their own agency in school. One such survey we know of asks students about their sense of agency in reading and writing (Vaughn et al., 2020) and is a valuable resource in your assessment toolkit.

Typical problems we see when it comes to students and their agency

Supporting student agency is more challenging for students than just completing a worksheet. When we invite students into the curriculum and work to foster their agency, as one of our school collaborators states, "they are drivers not just passengers." In other words, students are asked to engage differently than what they may be accustomed to when it comes to their learning. They are required to engage in higher level thinking and engage in complex decision-making in pursuit of their learning goals. Consider the above example where sixth graders led others in the creation of their own animated short videos. During these lessons, students were actively engaged in creating scripts, applying a variety of composing skills, as well as collaboratively working with others to complete tasks. This type of learning is dynamic and requires that students are no longer passive and follow along to teacher-directed instruction.

Students may be reluctant to share and may view activities where they are invited to share their voice in the classroom as some type of trick. We see this repeatedly in schools. We ask students what they want and then for a variety of reasons, we may not honor what they've asked. In many cases, students do not have faith in a system that has repeatedly denied them agency. Schools have historically denied agency to many students, families, and communities--particularly students from historically underrepresented populations and backgrounds. Many parents and communities have experienced trauma in their educational experiences.

Working to repair these tensions is multifaceted and requires time, learning, and commitment. One of the most important strategies toward fostering student agency is to include families and communities in the reading vision process as well. We encourage schools to send the message to families and communities that they are their child's first teacher and that they are essential partners in the process. Teachers can ask parents and families to create a family reading vision where families can write about the practices that they do when it comes to reading and what they would like for their child to accomplish when it comes to reading.

Instructional approaches to support student agency

Student agency is becoming a more well known concept in the field of education. Unfortunately, it is not necessarily a concept we explicitly talk about in teacher preparation or during professional development. Yet, it is one of the most foundational aspects of developing effective reading instruction and lifelong readers.

Table 6.1. Books to Discuss Agency

Title and Author	Genre and Suggested Grade Level
Stuck by Oliver Jeffers	Fantasy/k-3rd
The Girl and the Bicycle by Mark Pett	Realistic fiction k/3rd
After the Fall by Dan Santat	Fantasy/k-5th
Drum Dream Girl by Margarita Engle	Biographical fiction/k-5th
New Kid by Jerry Craft	Realistic fiction, graphic novel 4th–8th
El Deafo by Cece Bell	Biographical fiction, graphic novel 4th–8th

Let's consider some targeted ways to structure classroom environments that foster student agency. Here, we provide texts we believe can spark conversations with students about their agency and can ignite ways to help students in directing their own learning. See Table 6.1.

Additionally, there are resources that you can use to assess and evaluate students' agency. One particular assessment is the Student Agency Profile (Vaughn et al., 2020) that has specific questions for students to answer about their agency when it comes to reading and writing. This tool can be used to create a classroom profile as well as an individual profile for each student.

Additionally, the following instructional frameworks and activities can help to support opportunities for student agency.

Project based learning

Think about including research projects based on actively engaging students in something that interests them. Project based learning can encourage student agency as well as a variety of literacy skills where students can practice these skills in authentic ways. For example, ask students about a local topic or issue of concern for them. Scaffold learning with students and guide them to create their own culminating project. In one partner school, the second grade class, after realizing that many of the students at the school lacked books at home, researched how to create a little library outside of their school. The teacher read, *Little Libraries Big Heroes* (Paul, 2019), and the class began researching how to create a little library in front of their school. Projects like this that stem from students' ideas and passions can foster student agency (Vaughn et al., 2020).

Multimodal learning

Invite students into different ways to share their knowledge. Model skills using a variety of formats (audio, visual, as well as written), to encourage students to use a variety of tools to share what they know. One third grade teacher we know encourages this type of flexibility by asking students to recommend books. Students are encouraged to work with a partner or independently and choose how they want to share knowledge learned. Some students create a powerpoint, others create an movie, while others create a poster sharing what aspects of the book they liked and why. At the end of each month, the class has a celebration party where students' work is displayed, and students have the opportunity to share what they learned with the class.

Approaches to supporting student agency when talking with parents

Many of the same strategies used in the classroom to support student agency can be applied at home. We hear from parents that their child is disinterested in reading the minute they get through the front door. We understand and as parents, have been there ourselves. However, one of the strategies to encourage agency is to provide multiple opportunities for children to engage with a variety of texts and for a variety of purposes. For example, Marcus, Margaret's son, is seven and is crazy about anything Mario brothers and Nintendo Switch related. Because she is unskilled at playing, she invited him to share about how to play Mario Brothers, who the characters are, and the stories behind each of the missions. In this experience, Marcus had agency. He was able to decide how he shared his knowledge and was positioned as someone who was knowledgeable about the topic. He found several game manuals, read about the different characters, and went to the library to research nonfiction texts about games. Over several weeks, he worked on reading these materials and decided to make a book about the characters for Margaret to learn more about the game.

In order to invite parents into support their child's reading agency, focus on the following:

1. Reading is reading is reading. Many times, we hear from parents who are discouraged about what their child is reading. They share that their child is rereading *Waiting isn't easy*, (Willems, 2010) again and again

or they are reading yet another graphic novel. We want to encourage rereading of all types of texts as this is what real readers do. This openness supports their agency.

2. Invite parents to think of an idea/concern in their house or community and frame this with their child as an opportunity. For example, does the local park have litter? Invite your child to think about what they can do. Encourage parents to have the same types of conversations that you have with students during the day to problem solve. What can we do? Why, and what do you think?

3. Provide resources and access to materials so that all students and families can have access to materials. For example, work with the local library to develop a summer reading program or talk with your school's administration about developing a lending library option for the summer. Some school partners work with the local library to deliver books and resources throughout the summer months. Learn about what resources are available in your community to help provide access to materials and resources for students and families.

In addition to encouraging daily reading of texts of their child's choice, encourage parents and families to focus on a project that they can do together that is led by their child. This can be from creating a recycling bin in the house to planning a menu for the week. Agency requires that students see themselves as capable meaning makers. By structuring opportunities where their child can see themselves as knowledgeable contributors, this can encourage and foster a sense of agency. Ultimately, supporting student agency involves thinking about supporting students' dispositions, motivations, and how they are positioned. In other words, student agency involves supporting students' ideas, interests, as well as providing structured opportunities where they have a voice and choice in what they are learning.

Reflective questions

1. What does student agency mean to you and how will you implement it in your daily practice?

2. What are some of the linguistic strengths that families have that you can incorporate into your classroom? Are there ways you can invite students' families into your classroom to foster student agency?

3. Think about what your reading vision and the specific practices you will include to support your reading vision and how these practices align with student agency.

References

Bell, C. (2014). *El deafo*. Abrams.
Card, S. (2021). *Ender's becoming*. Tor Science Fiction.
Craft, J. (2019). *New kid*. Quill Tree Books.
Engle, M. (2015). *Drum dream girl: How one girl's courage changed music*. Houghton Mifflin Harcourt.
Gambrell, L. B. (1996). Creating classroom cultures that foster reading motivation. *Reading Teacher, 50*, 14–25.
Jeffers, O. (2011). *Stuck*. Philomel Books.
Miller, S., Stallings, S., Massey, D., & Metzger, S. R. (2022). A lesson in motion stays in motion: If students lead, will teachers follow?. *Phi Delta Kappan, 104*(4), 48–53.
Paul, M. (2019). *Little libraries, big heroes*. Clarion Books.
Pett, M. (2014). *The girl and the bicycle*. Simon and Schuster.
Santat, D. (2017). *After the fall* (How Humpty Dumpty got back up again). Roaring Book Press.
Vaughn, M. (2013). Examining teacher agency: Why did Les leave the building? *New Educator, 9*(2), 119–134.
Vaughn, M. (2014). The role of student agency: Exploring openings during literacy instruction. *Teaching and Learning: The Journal of Natural Inquiry & Reflective Practice, 28*(1), 4–16.
Vaughn, M. (2016). Re-envisioning literacy in a teacher inquiry group in a Native American context. *Literacy Research and Instruction, 55*(1), 24–47.
Vaughn, M. (2018). Making sense of student agency in the early grades. *Phi Delta Kappan, 99*(7), 62–66.
Vaughn, M. (2020a). What is student agency and why is it needed now more than ever. Student agency: Theoretical implications for practice [themed journal issue]. *Theory Into Practice, 59*(2), 109–118.
Vaughn, M. (2020b). Where to from here: Fostering agency across landscapes. Student agency: Theoretical implications for practice [themed journal issue]. *Theory Into Practice, 59*(2), 234–243.
Vaughn, M. (2021). *Student agency in the classroom: Honoring student voice in the curriculum*. Teachers College Press.
Vaughn, M., & Massey, D. (2021). *Teaching with children's literature: Theory to practice*. Guilford Press.
Vaughn, M., Premo, J. T., Sotirovska, V., & Erickson, D. (2020). Evaluating agency in literacy using the Student Agency Profile (StAP). *The Reading Teacher, 73*(4), 1–20.
Willems, M. (2010). *Gerald and Piggie (series)*. Hyperion Books for Children.

Part III
Instructional approaches

· 7 ·

WHAT CAN YOU DO TO STRENGTHEN PHONEMIC AWARENESS AND PHONICS?

Why are some children already considered behind in kindergarten? Many young children enter school with a strong vocabulary as well as understanding how words connect to create sentences. In addition, children may have a general idea of phonemes, or an understanding that sounds connect overall to language (Yopp & Yopp, 2000). They may understand that to say a sentence, they must use words. But even this is an abstract concept for many young children, and they may not fully comprehend what makes a word an actual word. Many young children enter school without *phonemic awareness*, or the understanding that individual letters have specific sounds and that these sounds are connected to how words are put together and form into how we speak and read words. Consider a concrete example of this. For a young child, when they hear the word hat, most children understand that a hat is something you put on your head. But they may be unaware that the word hat is also a series of individual phonemes or sounds, *h/a/t*, and that each sound can be represented by a distinct letter. Understanding phonemes and having phonemic awareness are a prerequisite for phonics (e.g., letter and sound relationships). Fortunately, we know from across the research that there are specific, targeted ways to strengthen phonemic awareness and phonics in children, particularly in the early grades.

Research on phonemic awareness and phonics

In order to understand the research, it is helpful to understand specific terms and how these terms are related to one another. Table 7.1 includes a list of terms that you will encounter in this chapter and in many reading curricula and assessments.

The importance of these terms is that they are the building blocks of what it takes to learn to read. Notice that phonics is only one small part of the overall picture depicted in Figure 7.1.

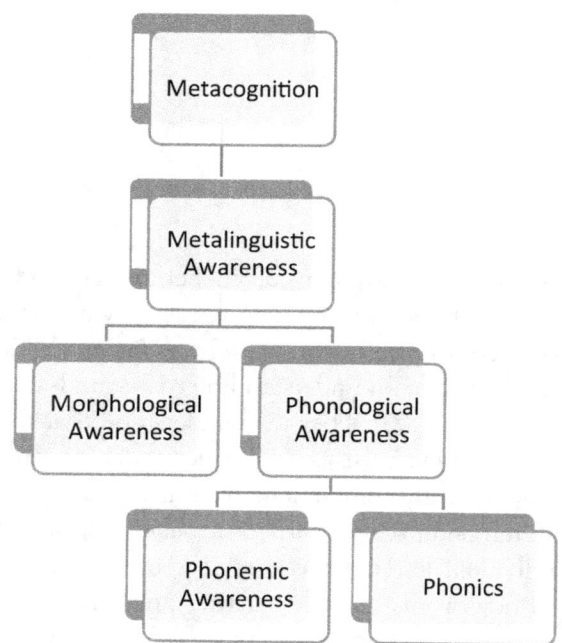

Figure 7.1. Relationship of Terms

Phoneme: a phoneme is the smallest part of a letter, or the specific sound of the letter. For example, the letter m makes the sound mmm, or the letter d, makes the sound /d/. It is the smallest part of the letter and the smallest unit of speech in words.

Phonemic awareness: is the ability of having the awareness of phonemes or sounds (i.e., that specific letters hold specific properties and have distinct units of sound associated with them). Students do not necessarily know what letters make certain sounds, but they are able to differentiate and manipulate sounds. Students who possess this awareness can identify that the word cap has the individual sounds c/a/p. As children become more skilled in their awareness, they can manipulate the individual phonemes to create new words. For example, when they hear the word pot, they can swap out the /p/ sound and replace it with the consonant blend sound, /sl/.

Phonological awareness: Phonological awareness is an umbrella term, as visualized in table Figure 7.1. Phonological awareness includes phonemic awareness, rhyming, and identifying individual words in sentences. For example, students can hear alliteration, know word boundaries, and the parts of words (i.e., syllables, onsets, rimes). Students who have phonological awareness can identify individual words within a sentence. These students know that in the sentence, *I can see the dog*, there are five different words. Moreover, there are individual letter sounds in the words that when connected together create a word. Students who have this awareness can identify the number of syllables that they hear in a word. For example, students can identify that in the word bicycle, there are three syllables which include bi/cy/cle. They can verbally separate the onset from a rime. For example, in the word, "cat," students who have phonological awareness can identify the "c" as the onset and the "at," as part of the rime. These students can then verbally switch out a "m" and "r" to make the words "mat" and "rat."

Metalinguistic awareness is an all-encompassing word that includes the awareness of structures of the language, including sounds (as in phonological awareness) as well as morphemes (morphemic awareness) (Nagy & Scott, 2000). It also implies the ability to manipulate components of language such as phonemes (sounds) and morphemes (meaning parts such as un- or -dict).

Understanding these terms and how they relate to building metacognition and metalinguistic awareness in children is critical when preparing to teach children how to read. We recommend that these skills are taught explicitly (Duffy, 2009) and with culturally relevant and engaging texts and materials (Vaughn & Massey, 2021). Further, we encourage you to think carefully about how you balance phonemic awareness with morphological awareness so that students can become more metacognitive of what they do as they read.

What is the importance of phonemic awareness?

Phonemic awareness is essential as children begin to learn to read. Students with phonemic awareness have the ability to break down small parts of words and also blend or put words together to make words. It allows children to move from the understanding that letters in the alphabet have sounds to being able to put together (blend) new words. Think of phonemic awareness like you would when using Legos to build a structure. Individually the Legos have their own properties, they are a certain color and shape and by themselves possess certain qualities and characteristics. When you put one Lego with another they can develop into a new shape or structure. The same occurs when you take them apart. This idea of blending and pulling apart Legos is much like manipulating individual letter sounds and combinations to create words. The complexity involved in creating words signals that children must possess this awareness as they advance toward reading. For example, without putting the right Lego piece together with another that it should fit, the structure may collapse or morph into something that was different than what was intended.

Some researchers state that phonemic awareness is the sole path toward providing the building blocks and the primary skills needed to ensure that a child can read successfully (Moats, 2019) whereas others emphasize a whole approach to teaching children these building blocks (Goodman, 1992). Some emphasize that language development (Allington, 2001) or the ability of young children to manipulate and use language and vocabulary, is what is needed. Others outline that understanding the role of play (Roskos et al., 2010), as well as young children's experiences with reading and writing, inform how equipped a reader will be as they learn to read (Gee, 2001).

Everyone is right. In other words, one singular method will not work for all children but understanding the varying layers of metalinguistic awareness and how to teach these elements in explicit and adaptive ways is vital. There is increased pressure to find the perfect method for teaching reading. Undoubtedly, the quest for finding this silver bullet has been around for decades and decades. Depending on which researcher, teacher, or publisher you talk to, the approach varies. However, what we do know is that adaptability and flexibility are essential when teaching reading. Think of your own experience with learning to read. You may have learned to read through learning strategies like, "sounding it out," or you may have been exposed to a wide variety of texts and learned to read by rereading predictable texts. In our experience, as we have shared, no two children are alike when it comes to reading. The one common thread is that explicit teaching of skills is required and that teachers need to know a variety of strategies and approaches to support students' metalinguistic awareness.

Explicit teaching of targeted skills (e.g., phonemes, consonant blends, digraphs, phonemic awareness) means that teachers use explicit instructional strategies and methods to teach these skills. In other words, teachers show students explicitly how to do the specific, targeted skill. In this way, the teaching is targeted with clear objectives, teacher modeling, and explicit skills are discussed in such a way that students can see the task clearly. What does explicit teaching look like in the context of early reading instruction? Consider the following example of a kindergarten teacher and how she applied explicit and adaptive teaching in the context of her reading lesson. In the kindergarten classroom, the teacher read aloud a predictable text that had the sentences, "I see a cat. I see a bat." The teacher highlighted the word family, "at" and continued reading the text aloud and identifying these word patterns. After the read aloud, the teacher asked students to practice writing words with this word family on their whiteboards. Students then created sentences using this word family. Such an example outlines how the skills are taught explicitly to students.

Instructional approaches to teaching phonics

How do we explicitly teach phonics? Consider how the teacher who outlines explicitly the digraph being taught. In the lesson, the teacher tells students, "Look at these two letters, 's' and 'h'" and writes these two letters on the board. She says,

> When we put these two letters together, we create the sound /sh/. We can see the /sh/ in the following words:
>
> show   sheep   ship

The teacher then pairs this explicit lesson with a read aloud that has the /sh/ highlighted in the story. As the teacher reads, she asks students to write down the /sh/ sound every time they see it and hear it as she reads aloud the story on their whiteboards and markers. In this way, the teacher is explicitly telling students the word pattern, explaining how the digraph is made, and then engages students in practicing identifying the pattern just taught.

In many early grade classrooms (k-2nd) grade we see the following approaches used to teach phonics. These include structured literacy activities where students can engage in meaningful activities to practice building letter and sound relationships.

1. Word sorts: Children are given a series of different letter and sound relationships and are asked to build and create words according to the letter and sound properties. For example, children sort a series of words where they are identifying the pattern ai and ay. Children sort the words into like vowel pattern categories:

    wait   slay
    bait   play
    train hay

2. Making words activities: Children are given letters and create various letter and word relationships. An example includes identifying word families and having students create words with the same short vowels:

    -an
    can
    sand
    man
    plant
    hand

3. Interactive read alouds: Much like in the above example, the teacher explicitly teaches a letter/word combination to the class and then includes this in a read aloud. The read aloud could be with a text, song, a video, or another material that highlights the letter/sound relationship. See the following table with some of our favorite texts to use during read alouds for teaching phonics.

The goal across these sample activities is that phonics is taught explicitly to students. Students segment different phonemes and build a variety of words applying the particular letter/sound relationship being identified.

Table 7.1. Books to Teach Skills

Title and Author	Phono. Awareness	Word Patterns	Phonics	Fluency
There's a Wocket in my Pocket by Dr. Seuss		X		
The Alphabet Tree by Leo Lionni	X			
You Read to Me, I Read to You series by Mary Ann Hoberman				X
The Bug in the Jug Wants a Hug by Brian P. Cleary		X	X	
Yo! Yes? By Chris Raschka	X			X
The Nice Mice in the Rice by Brian P. Cleary	X	X	X	
Gerald and Piggie series by Mo Willems				X
Q & U Call it Quits by Stef Wade		X	X	
Tanka Tanka Skunk! By Steve Webb		X	X	
It's a Book by Lane Smith				X
Hooway for Wodney Wat by Helen Lester	X		X	
I Love Lemonade by Mark and Rowan Sommerset				X

What are some common challenges we see in students when teaching these outlined skills and what can we do?

Although children may experience a variety of difficulties when learning these outlined skills, there are some common challenges readers experience. We outline these next and talk about practical strategies to support students:

Phonemic awareness

Although many students acquire phonemic awareness based on their experiences at home and school by the middle of first grade (roughly about 80–85%) (Chapman, 2003) some students may continue to struggle with obtaining this awareness. Ongoing monitoring and assessing children in kindergarten and first grade to ensure that they have these skills is vital. What can be done if children struggle with this early awareness? Provide targeted, structured teaching of identified skills that students lack. Provide access to materials. Ensure that students have access to culturally relevant and appropriate materials. Encourage opportunities for oral language development. Model how to ask questions and respond to questions when thinking and talking. Conduct think alouds and encourage children to play around with words in a variety of ways from using play-based approaches, like dramatic play, as well as other meaningful and relevant tasks (e.g., creating lists, rereading poems with targeted letter/word patterns).

As you can see, there are many skills that children need to develop that are building blocks to reading. Many scholars outline how the building blocks of learning to read are along a spectrum where students can progress. Encouraging the following areas can strengthen these early literacy skills.

- Rhyming and alliteration
- Sentence fragmenting
- Syllables, blending, and segmenting
- Onsets and rimes-differentiating the different phonemes as well as blending and segmenting

Transfer of skills

One concern we hear from teachers and parents is that children are happy to do standalone worksheets and activities on isolated skills, but they can't seem to transfer the isolated phonics instruction they've learned to "real reading." There is no easy answer to solving this particular challenge. However, we do offer a few suggestions. Remember all of the biology vocabulary words you learned in high school? Probably not. When we teach isolated words or skills disconnected from authentic learning opportunities, it becomes almost impossible for that learning to become part of our schema. Schema describes a pattern of thought that organizes different concepts. Put simply, it's a way for our brain to organize what we learn and put it into long term memory.

One thing we can do to build schema about words is to use authentic texts for students. when learning the word family "at," teachers can read aloud books that have this word pattern. For example, *Stellaluna* (Cannon, 1993) is about a bat who searches for her mom. Integrating a science-related unit on bats, to connect thinking about the word pattern, "at" can help students make deep connections to words and word patterns.

Additionally, modeling to students using read alouds and sentence frames (i.e., Look at the . . .) with specific words and patterns helps students make connections when they read. One concern we hear from teachers is that many of the books to teach phonics explicitly just aren't that engaging for kids. We suggest using a variety of materials to supplement curricular programs to bolster student engagement and interest in reading. Much like with the *Stellaluna* example, teachers can also pair high interest read alouds with word patterns that their students are learning. We recommend combining decodable books that emphasize regular patterns with more authentic texts where the words are more natural.

How do you assess phonics?

As we outline in our approach to assessment in previous chapters, assessing phonics can be understood in similar ways to other forms of assessment when it comes to literacy. We focus on our framework of assessment which includes observations, interviews, and artifacts/testing. For example, when considering how to assess phonemic awareness and students' phonics knowledge, we encourage observations when teachers watch children closely, listening to language, and how students use language. Are their vowel sounds correct and systematic? Students might have an accent or a dialect, but their short "a" sounds should be the same across short "a" words. Are they using endings in words or are they leaving off inflected endings such as -ed or -s? How are they using letters and sounds when writing? We can learn much from our observations of children when it comes to how they manipulate and use words. Similarly, we encourage engaging children in conversations and listening to students as they talk with one another. Rich conversations can happen when we ask students to tell us about their writing. Sitting next to a child and asking them to read what they've written or talk about a drawing provides insight into child's development of language, phonemic awareness, and phonics.

Using informal assessments like listening to how students converse with one another as well as more formal observations found in many curricular programs can help you assess phonemic awareness. Such tests gauge students' use of alphabetic principles as well as their ability to blend and rhyme words. Regardless of the publisher, most phonemic awareness tests include asking the following types of questions:

Phoneme identification:
What sound does the letter "s" make?
Phoneme matching:
Which words have similar sounds?
Phoneme isolating:
What is the beginning sound of the word cat?
What is the middle sound of the word cat?
What is the ending sound of the word cat?
Phoneme blending and segmenting:
When you put these sounds together, d/o/g/ what word does it make?
When you hear the word cat, what individual sounds do you hear?
Phoneme manipulation:
Can you say the word "jet" without the "j" sound? (correct answer: et)
Can you say the word "pig" without the "g" sound? (correct answer: pi)
Can you switch the first letter in cat to create a new word? So, for example, change the /c/ and put a /m/ to make a new word. What is the new word?

We also encourage other types of assessments such as assessing how students use print. For example, asking students to point to the front and the back of the book as well as identifying the title, a letter, and a word in a book are important tasks to do with children in the primary grades. You can probably gather that if children are able to point to the front and back of the book as well as identifying the title of a book that they have likely been exposed to books and materials. Alternatively, if children struggle to locate these concepts in texts, then they may have had minimal exposure. Other types of assessments to measure students' phonics knowledge are typically outlined by the school district and may vary. For the most part, these assessments focus on students' knowledge of how to connect letters to sounds and span across a continuum of higher leveled skills of manipulating phonemes.

Partnering with families

As we have discussed in previous chapters, it is important to acknowledge children and families' funds of knowledge (Moll et al., 1992). Children and families have funds of knowledge that include rich experiences, cultures, languages, and out of school lives. As educators, we must view children and families from a strength-based and asset-oriented approach. What might this look like in classrooms?

1. Invite children and families to share stories and experiences about their lives in the classroom.
2. Collaborate with parents and guardians to include culturally relevant materials and texts in the classroom utilizing students and families' first languages.
3. Include culturally relevant texts and materials in the classroom to teach the skills outlined in this chapter (i.e., phonemes, consonant blends, digraphs).
4. Recognize that families' literacy practices are essential in the classroom. This could be implemented in various ways from creating family book projects where families share important stories and share with the class to creating opportunities afterschool where families can share stories and experiences with others in the class.

In summary, it is essential to build phonological awareness in students using a variety of high-interest and engaging materials and activities. As highlighted in this chapter, phonemic awareness, phonological awareness, and building children's metalinguistic awareness helps children on their journey of becoming a reader. Without building these essential early skills, children will more than likely struggle when it comes to reading. We promote systematic and explicit phonics instruction where teachers model specific skills to students. By systematic, we recommend that letters and sounds are taught in an organized and systematic manner. By explicit, we reference that teachers use direct instructional methods to teaching letter and sound relationships to students.

Reflective questions

1. What essential information from this chapter would you want to share with parents? Why these aspects?

2. Why is explicit teaching of targeted skills critical when teaching these foundational reading skills? What are the potential gaps students may have if not taught these skills explicitly?

3. Revisit your reading vision. How can you incorporate these skills into aspects of your reading vision?

References

Allington, R. L. (2001). *What really matters for struggling readers: Designing research-based reading programs.* Longman.

Cannon, J. (1993). *Stellaluna* (Vol. 108). Houghton Mifflin Harcourt.

Chapman, M. L. (2003). Phonemic awareness: Clarifying what we know. *Literacy Teaching and Learning, 7,* 91–114.

Cleary, B. P. (2009a). *The clown in a gown drives the car with a star.* Millbrook Press.

Cleary, B. P. (2009b). *The nice mice in the rice.* LernerClassroom.

Duffy, G. G. (2009). *Explaining reading: A resource for teaching concepts, skills, and strategies.* Guilford Press.

Gee, J. (2001). Reading, language abilities, and semiotic resources: Beyond limited perspectives on reading. In J. Larson (Ed.), *Literacy as snake oil: Beyond the quick fix* (pp. 7–26). Peter Lang.

Goodman, K. S. (1992). Why whole language is today's agenda in education. *Language Arts, 69*(5), 354–363.

Hoberman, M. A. (2010). *You read to me, I'll read to you (series).* Little, Brown Books for Young Readers.

Lester, H. (2003). *Hooway for Wodney wat.* Houghton Mifflin Harcourt.

Lionni, L. (1968). *The alphabet tree.* Knopf Books for Young Readers.

Moats, L. (2019). Structured literacy: Effective instruction for students with dyslexia and related reading difficulties. *Perspectives on Language and Literacy, 45*(2), 9–10.

Moll, L. C., Amanti, C., Neff, D., & Gonzalez, N. (1992). Funds of knowledge for teaching: Using a qualitative approach to connect homes and classrooms. *Theory Into Practice, 31*(2), 132–141.

Nagy, W., & Scott, J. (2000). Vocabulary processes. In M. Kamil, P. Mosenthal, P. D. Pearson, & R. Barr (Eds.), *Handbook of reading research, 3.* (pp. 269–284). Lawrence Erlbaum Associates.

Raschka, C. (1993). *Yo! Yes?.* Orchard Books.

Roskos, K. A., Christie, J. F., Widman, S., & Holding, A. (2010). Three decades in: Priming for meta-analysis in play-literacy research. *Journal of Early Childhood Literacy, 10*(1), 55–96.

Seuss, T. D. (1974). *There's a wocket in my pocket* (Vol. 18). Random House Books for Young Readers.

Smith, L. (2010). *It's a book.* Roaring Book Press.

Sommerset, R., & Sommerset, W. (2016). *I love lemonade.* Candlewick.

Vaughn, M., & Massey, D. (2021). *Teaching with children's literature: Theory to practice.* Guilford Press.

Wade, S. (2021). *Q and u call it quits.* Quill Tree Books.

Webb, S. (2004). *Tanka tanka skunk.* Random House.

Willems, M. (2010). *Gerald and Piggie (series).* Hyperion Books for Children.

Yopp, H., & Yopp, R. (2000). Supporting phonemic awareness development in the classroom. *The Reading Teacher, 54*(2), 130–143.

· 8 ·

WHAT CAN YOU DO TO STRENGTHEN DECODING AND FLUENCY?

During an observation in a second grade classroom, a student excitedly shared, "I can read really fast! Listen to me read, watch!" As Margaret sat and listened to the student read, she then asked her to share what the passage was about. In other words, Margaret wanted to know if she comprehended what she read. She remembered some of the characters' names but struggled to remember anything beyond that. Fluency is important but we want to ensure that the purpose of reading is not reading a text fast but to understand and comprehend what is read.

Research on decoding and fluency

Decoding and oral reading fluency are considered important dimensions of reading (Allington, 1983; Collins, 1982). One of the common occurrences that happens when learning to read is that children will come across a word they do not know. Decoding is the ability to apply what is known about letter and sound relationships and patterns to figure out words that are unknown (Moats, 1998). Explicit teaching of decoding requires that teachers model to students how to decode. Students must be able to decode in order to fully comprehend what they read. Additionally, if a student struggles with decoding as they read, they will be unable to read the text fluently. As Pikulski and Chard (2005) stated, "If attention is drained by decoding words, little or no capacity is available for the attention-demanding process of comprehending. Therefore, automaticity of decoding—a critical component of fluency—is essential for high levels of reading achievement" (p. 511). Decoding asks students to look at a word and know how to segment its parts to read the word. Students must master the ability to decode to fully become fluent. In other words, students must decode words automatically (often referred to as reading automaticity) where they know the word immediately and become automatic in the decoding process. Watch a new reader as they practice decoding. You will see them look within a word, look for what word patterns they see in the word, and then work to decipher or decode the word. Then, observe a more fluent reader. This reader will automatically decode as they read. They rarely stop to look within a word to figure out unknown words, instead they decode automatically as they read.

Fluency is another vital skill that readers must possess. According to the National Reading Panel, fluency is the ability of students to read text with accuracy, at an appropriate rate, and good expression (NICHD, 2000). When students read fluently, they are more likely to comprehend what is they read at a better rate than those students who do not read fluently. For example, students who are less fluent tend to apply a variety of behaviors that may impede their comprehension as well as their fluency. These readers may pause, look back, reread, and read at a slower pace. According to Walczyk and Griffith-Ross (2007), in their research of third, fifth, and seventh graders, students who were more fluent consistently maintained higher comprehension than those students who were less fluent. Similarly, Griffith and Rasinski (2004) found that as the author (Griffith), a fourth grade teacher, incorporated reader's theater, partner reading, and timed reading practices, into her reading instruction, her students consistently became more fluent and performed higher on reading assessments. Her reflection of a focus on fluency is noteworthy:

> I have also learned that reading fluency can be taught in a variety of ways. Teachers interested in making fluency an integral part of their instructional curriculum for reading should rely on certain key principles in designing such instruction: Fluency requires opportunities for students to hear fluent, expressive, and meaningful reading from their teacher, their parents, and their classmates; fluency requires opportunities for students to practice reading texts multiple times; fluency requires opportunities for students to be coached in fluent, expressive, and meaningful reading by their teacher and their classmates; and fluency requires opportunities for students to engage in meaningful and critical discussions of the texts they read and meaningful

performances of the texts they practice. How these principles are turned into actual practice depends on the individual teacher. In my own classroom, I found that these principles came to life in Readers Theatre, timed reading, and partner reading and that they had a positive impact on my students' reading development. (p. 136)

There are three distinct components of fluency which include:

Accuracy: Also known as automaticity, it refers to the person's ability to read words in a text.
Rate: The speed a person reads.
Prosody and expression: Refers to stress, intonation, and pauses. Commonly known as "reading with feeling".

These outlined areas (i.e., accuracy, rate, and prosody/expression) comprise what we think of when we think of fluency (Rasinski, 2012) and are integral in supporting how to support students' ability to read naturally (Stecker et al., 1998).

Instruction on decoding

What does explicit modeling of instruction on decoding look like? In many cases, this type of teaching involves the teacher using a word, a poem or other type of text to model specific relationships to students. For example, a teacher might work with students on recognizing initial letter and sound relationships. A teacher might write the letters b and h and the word hat on the board and ask:

- "What sound does /b/ make?"
- "What sound does /h/ make?"
- "What is the letter that you see at the front of the word? What sound does that letter make? What letter is at the end of the word? What sound does that letter make?"

Effective teaching of reading means that teachers explicitly teach decoding to students. Students are provided with opportunities to:

1. Practice and apply knowledge of sound-letter relationships to learn a variety of decoding skills.

Table 8.1. Sound-letter Relationships

Phoneme (sound)	Location of Important Phoneme/beginning	Location of Important Phoneme/ending	Examples
/k/	c/k/ch	k/ck	can, kick, crook, rock
/p/	p	p	pot, top
/th/	th	the	there, bathe
/d/	d	d	dot, bed

2. Engage with materials such as texts, word games, and engaging materials to apply their knowledge of sound-letter patterns and explore a variety of sound-letter relationships.
3. Use a variety of strategies to gain meaning of a word including using the word parts and understandings of phonemes to confirm the meaning of words (e.g., shipping).
4. Apply knowledge and practice structural analysis practice, or the ability to look at distinct phonemes, syllables, and multisyllabic words to decode and understand words.

We recommend that teachers explicitly teach a variety of sound-letter relationships (found in Table 8.1) and common vowel patterns (sampled in Table 8.2).

Table 8.2. Common Vowel Patterns

Phoneme	Spelling	examples
/a/	a-e, ay, ai, ei, ea, ey, eigh	cake, may, bait, veil, steak, hey, sleigh
/e/	e, ee, ea, y, ie, e_e, ey, i_e, ei	be, keep, teach, plenty, yield, these, machine, receive
/i/	i_e, y, i, ie, igh, ye	lime, my, find, pie, night, bye

In addition to teaching these sound-letter relationships explicitly to students, we also recommend that students engage in meaningful activities to build these relationships on their own. Teachers and families can use a variety of activities to involve students in this process including:

- Games and activities both hands on and via technology where students can practice building, segmenting, and exploring a variety of sound-letter relationships.
- Reading materials including poetry, shortened passages that highlight specific sound-letter relationships. Students can interact with these materials to highlight, locate, and write down specific patterns and relationships.
- Tactile activities such as magnetic letters, and tiles, where students can build word families and patterns. Other ideas include having students write patterns and words in a tray filled with sand or shaving cream.
- Using bead slides where beads are put on pipe cleaners and as students say multisyllabic words, they slide down beads to represent the different sound parts.

Some common problems students have when it comes to decoding is connecting the skills and putting it into practice on their own. Additionally, some students may struggle in the following ways:

- Unsure of what sounds make particular word patterns.
- Know the sounds in isolation but struggle to connect the individual sounds to understand the entire word.
- Stamina- decoding takes stamina and sometimes children struggle with the act of decoding and then become disinterested in wanting to read because the task of decoding can take such a long time.
- Students do not read fluently, instead they read more in a robotic fashion.
- Guessing and more guessing because of a variety of the reasons outlined above.

When students struggle to decode, we often hear them say, "I'm no good at reading," and "I can't read," and even, "I hate reading!" Some children have specific learning challenges like dyslexia. According to the Mayo Clinic (n.d.),

> Dyslexia is a result of individual differences in areas of the brain that process language. Dyslexia is not due to problems with intelligence, hearing, or vision. Most children with dyslexia can succeed in school with tutoring or a specialized education program. Emotional support also plays an important role.

Students with dyslexia have difficulty decoding and identifying speech sounds. However, for many students, decoding can be explicitly taught in the ways we outline in this chapter. We encourage explicitly sharing with parents this information, especially the need to support decoding practices at home. This can be supported in a variety of ways.

An important teaching tool is talking with children about some of the words you encounter. For example, when reading aloud to students, you read the word 'monitor.' Explain what the word means and also show them the different parts of the word, for example, how part, "on" can be found in the word as well as other word parts like "it" and "or." Explain that these individual word parts connect to create this word.

In addition to talking about words informally, encourage children both in and out of school to write as often as possible. We first encourage students to use their best guess spelling which means that children listen to the sound that they hear and then write these words down. Then we use what they've written to build and explicitly teach individually focused lessons on the words they miss and also get right. Teachers must use explicit, systematic teaching practices to teach phonemes, and sound-letter relationships to increase students' ability both in reading and writing.

Instruction on fluency

Fluent readers read with appropriate speed, prosody (phrasing) and expression. When readers are fluent, they know words automatically, in that they no longer have to stop and decode words as they read. To build fluent readers, classrooms should be rich with a variety of texts, materials, and opportunities to read and practice reading fluently. Students should have opportunities to:

1. Read and reread a variety of texts, materials (i.e., plays, poems), and opportunities where they can read to the teacher, a partner, a small group, or as part of a larger group such as in choral reading.
2. Use authentic opportunities to read. Encourage students to read to others. For example, invite first grade students to read a book that they have reread several times to kindergartners. Encourage students to record themselves as they read so that they can then hear themselves read. We know several teachers who have students record short books

they've read and then use them as resources for students to listen to and enjoy.
3. Invite students to participate in reader's theater where they take a short play, poem, or passage, and practice and then perform for the class or another audience.

Much like in all aspects of effective teaching of reading, we encourage the use of systematic and explicit teaching of fluency. What does this look like? In the following we outline how to model fluent reading. First, we encourage the use of interesting, engaging passages, poems, books, and other materials to model to students how to read fluently. Second, fluent reading should include explicitly talking about how you change your rate of reading based on how difficult the text is and how you know when to pause by observing the punctuation. Third, reading aloud to students daily is vital. We encourage reading a variety of texts that are interesting, engaging, and culturally responsive, as well as from across a variety of genres and disciplines. Refer to the table of books we suggest for teaching these skills in Chapter 7 (Table 7.1).

Assessing decoding and fluency

The role of assessment is critical when teaching decoding and fluency with students. There are many assessments that are used to assess students in these areas. We once again focus on our framework assessment in this chapter which includes observations, interviews, and artifacts/testing. When observing, focus on what students are doing when they come across an unknown word as they read. Are they applying knowledge of sound-letter relationships? Are they guessing at a word? Ask students what they do when they come across an unknown word and why they use that particular strategy. We encourage the use of observation as a critical tool in all aspects of reading but especially as students are working to transfer what they know about sound-letter relationships and how they put this into practice.

In terms of the role of artifacts/testing, we want to focus on what the research outlines about effective ways to measure students' fluency as well as ways to assess how students are decoding and what areas of support are needed. Fluency assessments center around center on measuring the three areas outlined of fluency: accuracy, rate, and prosody/expression (Wolf & Katzir-Cohen, 2001). Although there are many ways to measure fluency from curricular assessments as well other standardized assessments, we instead turn to a measure that any teacher can assess using the National Assessment of Educational Progress Fluency Scale (NAEP, 2022). Teachers can assess students' fluency by giving them a one-minute timed reading passage and then assess how students perform according to this scale (See Table 8.3).

Table 8.3. National Assessment of Educational Progress Fluency Scale

Level 1/Non Fluent	Level 2/Non fluent	Level 3/Fluent	Level 4/Fluent
Reads primarily word-by-word. Occasional two-word or three-word phrases may occur but these are infrequent and/or they do not preserve meaningful syntax.	Reads primarily in two-word phrases with some three- or four-word groupings. Some word-by-word reading may be present. Word groupings may seem awkward and unrelated to larger context of sentence or passage	Reads primarily in three- or four-word phrase groups. Some small groupings may be present. however, the majority of phrasing seems appropriate and preserves the syntax of the author. Little or no expressive interpretation is present.	Reads primarily in larger, meaningful phrase groups. Although some regressions, repetitions, and deviations from text may be present, these do not appear to detract from the overall structure of the story. Preservation of the author's syntax is consistent. some or most of the story is read with expressive interpretation.

Another type of fluency assessment is as follows:

1. Select a reading passage for a targeted grade level that you want to see if the student is reading at a particular grade level. Set the timer for 60 seconds.
2. The students read aloud the passage and then mark down any words that caused hesitation or were skipped.
3. Mark the spot in the passage where the timer stops and where the student stopped.
4. Then count the words in the selection of the part of the passage that the word was read (this is called words per minute/WPM).
5. Then subtract the problem words from the WPM to determine the students' accuracy rate.
6. Divide the accuracy of the students' reading results from the WPM. This answer is the fluency percentage of the particular passage and the students' fluency rate. If the percentage is less than 75% then the student

is struggling with fluency and is still working on decoding. Eighty-eight percent can be determined as instructional level and 95% means that students are reading fluently independently.

These measures and ways to assess fluency can help to determine the three areas of fluency outlined in this chapter (i.e., accuracy, rate, and prosody/expression). As we share, building on students' decoding skills will lend itself to support students' fluency as well. If students are struggling with decoding skills, they will also struggle with fluency and the outlined aspects of fluency. We want to make sure that we engage in systematic explicit instruction.

Ultimately, decoding and fluency are about building towards readers who can comprehend what they read. Fluent readers can decode appropriately, allowing them to focus on comprehension, noticing more about the ideas and information presented in the text. Students develop skills according to their developmental abilities; however, we typically see that by the end of second grade, students have mastered decoding and are focused on reading fluently. This is the reason that if you enter a third grade classroom, you may see that the teacher is explicitly teaching comprehension skills and strategies to students. In other words, as students figure out and excel with decoding, they progress to a focus on learning to become more fluent. As they master fluency, they can focus their mental energy on comprehension.

Reflective questions

1. How can you use decodable texts to teach decodable skills? Look back at the images of texts in Chapter 1 and brainstorm targeted skills you can teach with these texts.

2. Create a game where students can practice building, segmenting, and exploring a variety of sound-letter relationships.

3. What knowledge from this chapter is essential to share with parents?

References

Allington, R. L. (1983). Fluency: The neglected reading goal. *The Reading Teacher, 36*(6), 556–561.

Collins, J. (1982). Discourse style, classroom interaction and differential treatment. *Journal of Reading Behavior, 14*(4), 429–437.

Griffith, L. W., & Rasinski, T. V. (2004). A focus on fluency: How one teacher incorporated fluency with her reading curriculum. *The Reading Teacher, 58*(2), 126–137.

Mayo Clinic. (n.d.) Dyslexia. Retrieved from https://www.mayoclinic.org/diseases-conditions/dyslexia/symptoms-causes/syc-20353552

Moats, L. C. (1998). Teaching decoding. *American Educator, 22*(1), 42–49.

NAEP. (2022). *NAEP report card: 2022 NAEP reading assessment.* Retrieved from https://www.nationsreportcard.gov/highlights/reading/2022/

National Institute of Child Health and Development (NICHD). (2000). Report of the National Reading Panel: Teaching children to read: An evidence-based assessment of the scientific research literature on reading and its implications for reading instruction (NIH Publication No. 00-4769). Washington, DC: U.S. Government Printing Office. Available at https://www.nichd.nih.gov/publications/pubs/nrp/pages/smallbook.aspx

Pikulski, J. J., & Chard, D. J. (2005). Fluency: Bridge between decoding and reading comprehension. *The Reading Teacher, 58*(6), 510–519.

Rasinski, T. V. (2012). Why reading fluency should be hot!. *The Reading Teacher, 65*(8), 516-522.

Stecker, S. K., Roser, N. L., & Martinez, M. G. (1998). Understanding oral reading fluency. In T. Shanahan & F. V. Rodriguez-Brown (Eds.), *47th yearbook of the National Reading Conference* (pp. 295–310). National Reading Conference.

Walczyk, J. J., & Griffith-Ross, D. A. (2007). How important is reading skill fluency for comprehension? *The Reading Teacher, 60*(6), 560–569.

Wolf, M., & Katzir-Cohen, T. (2001). Reading fluency and its intervention. *Scientific Studies of Reading, 5*(3), 211–239.

· 9 ·

WHAT CAN YOU DO TO STRENGTHEN STUDENTS' COMPREHENSION AND VOCABULARY?

Adam enjoyed learning to read. He eagerly read picture books such as the *Pete the Cat* series (Dean, 2015). When his primary grade teacher tested Adam, he scored well in fluency and decoding measures. But by the middle of fourth grade, Adam was struggling on reading tests. His mother noticed that he didn't seem to be paying attention to what he was reading. She also observed that Adam didn't want to go to the library or receive books as gifts. He liked some graphic novels and if he was asked to read at home, he read the same books over and over. His teacher noted that when Adam was asked to retell a story or passage, his retellings were often disjointed and out of order. He particularly struggled to retell nonfiction passages. When reading about state history, Adam was often off-task. In science, he relied on a partner to help him follow directions for hands-on activities. Adam said that he thought science and history were boring. Adam was clearly struggling with comprehension and vocabulary. These areas are critical for making meaning, yet some students experience difficulty making the transition from identifying words on a page and pronouncing them to using those words to learn information.

Research about reading comprehension and vocabulary

Comprehension is the act of making meaning. It is an internal thinking process that is influenced by prior knowledge and experiences. Vocabulary is also influenced by prior knowledge and ways of thinking. Vocabulary shares a reciprocal relationship with comprehension; that is, it influences one's ability to comprehend text. At the same time, an understanding of text may help the reader understand new vocabulary.

Reader's experiences

"What students *already know* about the content is one of the strongest indicators of how well they will learn new information relative to the content" (Marzano, 2004, p. 1). Scholars repeatedly emphasize the important role of background knowledge when developing students' comprehension of a particular topic (Guthrie, 2007). Additionally, prior knowledge and experiences shape students' ability to make inferences (Castells et al., 2021; Wolf & Potter, 2018). For example, imagine encountering the sentence, "Baking baklavas with Grandma requires a lot of patience but the reward is very tasty." If a student bakes at home with a family member and then reads a text about baking, the student can draw on the vocabulary used at home, the knowledge of a sequence of steps, and even sensory information such as smells. All of this knowledge allows students to make a different or more robust inference even if they do not know exactly what baklavas are compared with an inference from a student who has never baked at home.

Ways of thinking

While there are many ways that people think about text as they read (Pressley & Afflerbach, 1995), cognitive research has indicated that most readers regularly use a combination of 8–10 ways of thinking (Duffy, 2009). often called comprehension strategies. These ways of thinking include: monitoring understanding and using fix-up strategies, activating relevant prior knowledge, understanding text structure, reading/viewing with a purpose, creating sensory images (visual, audio), summarizing, making relevant connections, asking and answering questions of the text, making predictions/inferences, and evaluating text.

Each reader may use a different strategy or combination of strategies when encountering a text. The teacher's job is to facilitate this meaning making and seek to understand how the child is making meaning with the text, rather than simply look for particular interpretations of the text (Aukerman, 2008).

Students come to school with a variety of ways of thinking. They have been exposed to oral stories, movies, and books. For example, a student who loves trucks and equipment can often make connections between what she has listened to and what she sees outside at a construction site. She may be able to make predictions about what new equipment is used for based on her prior knowledge. What the student may lack is an awareness of her way of thinking. The self-awareness is important because it allows the students to identify what to try when they encounter difficulty in texts.

The author and the text

In any text, the author brings his or her own experiences and background knowledge to the text. The author uses particular styles of writing. These may influence the reader's comprehension. For example, if the author uses a lot of figurative language, students may struggle to understand what is really happening.

The point of considering readers' experiences, ways of thinking, and the author and text influences is that comprehension—the act of making meaning from text—is a complex process. Pearson and Cervetti (2017) observed that a reader's comprehension is still puzzling:

> Comprehension, or understanding, by its very nature, is a phenomenon that can only be observed indirectly. People tell us that they understood, or were puzzled by, or enjoyed, or were upset by a text. Or, more commonly, we quiz them on the text in some way. All of these tasks, however challenging or engaging they might be, are little more than the residue of the comprehension process itself. (p. 13)

Vocabulary

Vocabulary knowledge is also critical component of comprehension. Vocabulary predicts reading comprehension (Elleman & Oslund, 2019). The more words that a reader knows, the more likely the reader is to understand the text. Scott and colleagues (Scott et al., 2008) describe vocabulary's link to comprehension this way:

When students encounter an unfamiliar word in a text, the question is not whether they can come up with a definition for that word, but whether they know enough to continue reading with an adequate level of comprehension. Thus, word learning strategies must be coordinated with a sophisticated level of comprehension monitoring. (p. 192)

Children acquire vocabulary at an astounding rate, on average two to eight root words per day (Biemiller & Slonim, 2001). Most words are learned implicitly through repeated exposures in multiple contexts over time (Landauer & Dumais, 1997). That means that students need to read a lot and read widely in order to create the most conducive environment for learning new vocabulary words.

Unfortunately, large individual differences in vocabulary size exist in early readers and persist through elementary school (Biemiller & Slonim, 2001). Students from homes below or at the poverty level, can lag two years behind their average peers and four years behind those in the upper quartile on vocabulary knowledge.

Instruction to support comprehension and vocabulary

Students will face many challenges when learning comprehension and vocabulary skills (See Table 9.1). Knowing common patterns of challenges to students' comprehension, we can use the assessment framework to gather additional information about specific students. By focusing on the assessment framework of observation, conversation, artifacts/testing, we can gain valuable insight about where to begin with comprehension and vocabulary instruction.

Assessment

Starting with observations and conversations can help us focus on the student instead of only on the curriculum. Additionally, observation and conversation are critical to understand more about the background knowledge that students bring to the classroom.

Observation

We recommend starting with an Observation Protocol like that shared in Chapter 4. Begin creating a classroom profile of your students. Some teachers

Table 9.1. Challenges in Comprehension and Vocabulary

Challenge	Instructional Response
Students' lack background knowledge, including vocabulary.	Use assessment to understand the background knowledge that students bring to the text. Build background knowledge through shared class experiences. Include explicit instruction about how to monitor when background knowledge is interfering in understanding.
Students don't know that they do not understand the text.	Teach students to monitor their comprehension and be metacognitive through self-assessment and modeling how to think about reading.
Students focus on decoding and fluency at the expense of understanding.	Emphasize that text should make sense. Teach students how to vary their reading speed to support reading comprehension and reread with purpose. Do not ask students to read aloud until they have had an opportunity to read the text to themselves silently.
Students are not able to identify what is important in the text.	Focus on text structures. Text structures provide clear direction about what is important in the text. Text that is written as fictional narrative will include particular text elements that should be the focus.

explain that their students, "aren't reading yet." Observation Protocols are still important. For example, are the students looking at pictures? Are they talking about what's in the pictures? If they are, then they are reading! These reading-like behaviors signify what early readers do when they read. Gather a selection of wordless books from the school library. We know one teacher who worked with a librarian at a large public library. They agreed on a time and the teacher was able to check out all of the wordless books that the library system had available to encourage early readers.

Vocabulary knowledge can be observed when students are talking with one another, as well as when students are given written or verbal directions to follow. At first, listen to see if anything stands out as being different from other peers that is not explained with language differences. Over time, listen to see if they are beginning to use vocabulary that has been introduced in class.

Conversation

Begin to talk with students one at a time. This may take multiple weeks to complete. Let students know that you want to get to know them, and you will get to each one.

When you start the conversation with an individual student, pick one or two items from your observation protocol and tell the student what you noticed. For example, you might say, "I noticed that you picked up the book about bears and then put it back. Can you tell me why you did that?" Or, "I noticed that you started looking around about three minutes after you started to read. Did you know that you did that? Do you know why you did that?" Rather than being quick to judge students' motives, let them do as much explaining as they can. You might discover that they're always hungry in the middle of the morning or they realized they'd read that book before instead of that they lacked stamina or motivation to read.

Conversation is also an important way to gather information about their vocabulary usage. Remember that most tests will assess vocabulary by asking what a word means. However, prior knowledge and awareness of testing practices can advantage some children and disadvantage others. Pay attention to the words they use and the way they use them when they are speaking and begin noting questions you have about their vocabulary.

Additionally, focus on the metacognitive processes of vocabulary. Use a conversation or two to ask what they do when they come to a word that they do not understand. This will be a difficult question for some students; they will immediately think that you mean a word that they cannot pronounce. They may try to give answers that they think you want such as "Use context clues" without really knowing what that means or knowing how to apply it on their own. Look for authentic examples to ask students how they figure out what a sentence or word means when they aren't sure.

Artifacts/testing

After observation and conversation, invite the student to read to you. Instead of asking questions after they read, simply ask, "What were you thinking about as you read?" Answers will range from "nothing" to "I don't know" to a near-essay on how the world works. Again, your job is to listen and collect as much information as possible.

Eventually, you will begin testing. You may have tests that the curriculum or district requires. If not, you can use a running record and student retelling or reading inventory such as the *Qualitative Reading Inventory-7* (Leslie & Caldwell, 2021), to learn more about the students' reading. Ideally, the testing data should confirm or challenge what you are already seeing from your notes. If there is a discrepancy such as it seems like the student who had lots to tell

WHAT CAN YOU DO TO STRENGTHEN STUDENTS' COMPREHENSION

you about reading in a one on one conversation does poorly on the assessment, you'll want to repeat the process of observation and conversation.

Many teachers tell us that after conducting observations and conversations, they feel like the test is not giving them the full picture. For example, sometimes they find that students can read at a much higher level when it comes to books they choose compared with books that are chosen for them. Sometimes a passage requires very specific background knowledge to fully understand and this disadvantages some students.

Build conceptual knowledge and background knowledge

In order to build comprehension, students will need to know the meanings of many words. However, the research makes it clear that teachers can never teach students all the words they will need to know. In order to build both vocabulary knowledge and overall comprehension, it is important to focus on concepts, not just words in isolation.

Meanings of words are not just "known" or "unknown." Instead, there is a continuum of knowing words (Dale, O'Rourke, & Bamman, 1971), with gradations of understanding existing between the levels (Figure 9.1).

Consider how familiar you are with the following words. Assign each a level of knowledge.

Contranym   Zarf   Polysemy
Pedagogy   Problematize   Mullion

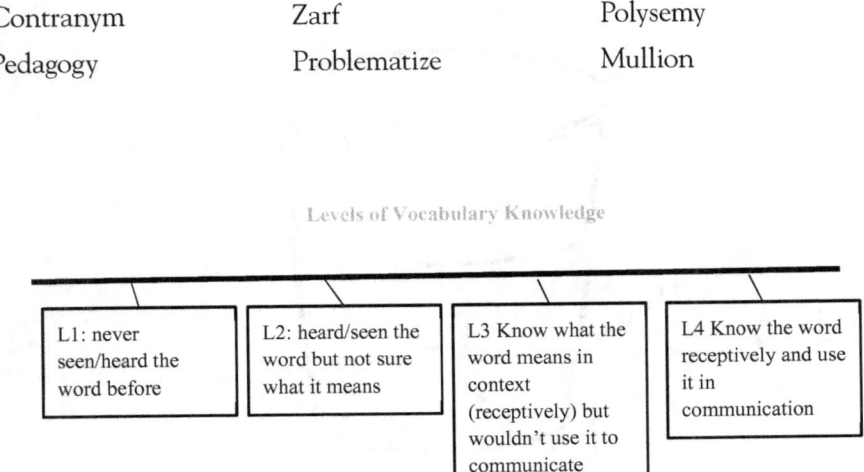

Figure 9.1. Four Levels of Vocabulary Knowledge

Chances are that you have different levels of understanding about these words. Consider the word zarf. You might have ranked this word as a Level 1 or Level 2 because it is unfamiliar. If we showed you an image of a disposable coffee cup with a cardboard sleeve (such as Figure 9.2) labeled with the word "zarf,", your reaction might be, "Oh, I didn't know it had a name other than sleeve." If you have ever used a disposable coffee cup, or seen others using them, zarf is easy to connect to the larger concept of coffee shops. In other words, you already have the conceptual knowledge and now you're adding a word that is connected to the conceptual knowledge.

If we considered individual words in isolation, it would be difficult to know what some of them meant. Consider the word "executive" in reference to the Executive Branch. This word is introduced in many primary grades' social studies curriculum. In order to understand what executive means in this context, students need to have a larger idea of the concept of democracy. They will need to add related words to their conceptual knowledge, as illustrated in Figure 9.3.

If our students do not have conceptual knowledge, or if they are trying to memorize words in isolation and they fail to attach the word to the correct concept, the words will be harder to learn and remember. Simply writing a definition on the board will not be enough for robust understanding. In order to help students learn more vocabulary, they need to know something about the larger concept. This builds the background and the word awareness they will need to comprehend complex texts. For example, building a visual such

Figure 9.2. Cup

WHAT CAN YOU DO TO STRENGTHEN STUDENTS' COMPREHENSION

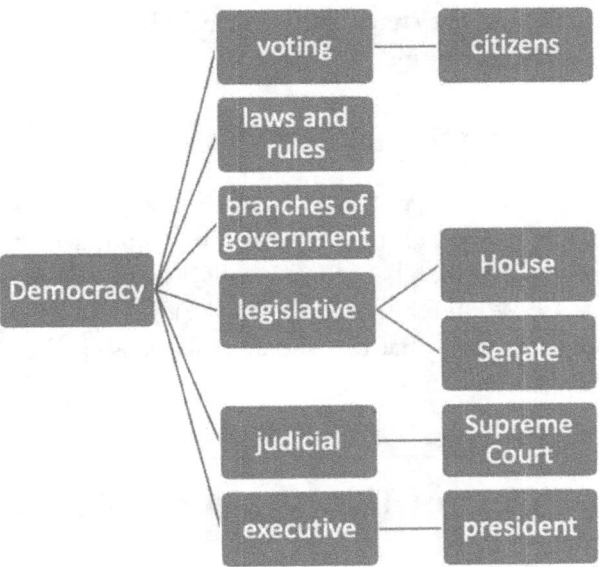

Figure 9.3. Conceptual Word Knowledge

as the one found in Figure 9.3 and displaying it as a reference in the room can help students build conceptual knowledge and specific awareness about individual words.

Knowing when it doesn't make sense: Monitoring and metacognition

Dixie once worked with a 14-year old student who told her he was a good reader. He paused, then asked with complete sincerity, "Does comprehension have something to do with reading? I'm not so good at comprehension but I'm a good reader."

Sometimes our students don't realize that texts should make sense. As strange as that sounds, many students have misconceptions about reading. They view reading as something to finish and so they read quickly, without varying their rate or monitoring their understanding. Some readers get so wrapped up in performing the reading—saying the words correctly and sounding fluent—that they fail to focus on the meaning. Many students making the switch from decodable or pattern texts to more authentic texts may struggle to attend to the meaning. Some older students think of themselves as poor at comprehension because they have not been taught how to think about the text and think about their thinking.

What do I teach first?

When thinking about the primary ways of thinking listed earlier, it can be difficult to know where to begin. The first way of thinking we suggest teaching is monitoring comprehension because this calls attention to the idea that texts should make sense. We use a Comprehension Flowchart (Figure 9.4) to help students attend to the idea that text should make sense and to focus on what to do if the text isn't making sense.

Ways of Thinking about Text

- Monitor understanding and use fix-up strategies
- Activate relevant prior knowledge
- Understand text structure
- Read/view with a purpose
- Create mental images (visual, audible, etc.)
- Summarize
- Make relevant connections
- Ask and answer questions of the text
- Make predictions/inferences
- Evaluate text

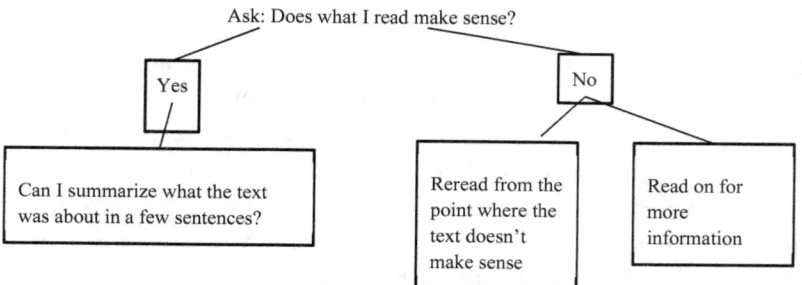

Figure 9.4. Comprehension Flowchart

WHAT CAN YOU DO TO STRENGTHEN STUDENTS' COMPREHENSION

After we emphasize that text should make sense and how to begin to monitor it with a protocol such as the Comprehension Flowchart, we introduce or review text structures. This helps students know what to pay attention to in the text. Table 9.2 summarizes the purposes for reading within the main text structures.

Table 9.2. Text Structure

Text Structure	Elements of Structure	Purpose for Reading within Structure
Narrative	Character, settings, conflicts, resolutions, tones, themes	Who are the characters? What are the settings? What are the conflicts and how are they resolved? What are the relationships between pattern elements? (e.g., What are the relationships between the characters? What is the relationship between the characters and the setting? Why did the characters experience conflict?)
Expository	Compare-contrast, descriptive, cause-effect, problem-solution, chronological, blended format	*Compare-contrast*: What things are being compared? What are the similarities and differences? *Description*: What is being described? What are the characteristics? *Cause-effect*: What are the causes? What are the effects? How are the causes and effects related? Could the causes result in different effects under different circumstances? *Problem-solution*: What are the problems? What are the solutions? How are or could the solutions be achieved? *Chronological*: What is the sequence of events? Why is the sequence important?
Poetry	Free verse, haiku, cinquain, concrete, couplet, limerick,	Why might the author have chosen poetry instead of another text format? How does the author use language, grammar, and mechanics to support the poem?

Following monitoring and text structure, we invite students to practice particular ways of thinking, such as summarizing or making connections, while simultaneously asking them to think metacognitively about their strategy use and vocabulary. Consider how the short text, *The New Marine*, helps the reader pull together multiple ways of thinking.

The New Marine

The newest Marine to the 5th Marine Regiment was tough. She could outrun all of the other soldiers. She could carry more weight in her pack than any of the men. She could even eat more than anyone else, especially if it was scrambled eggs, washed down with her favorite drink of Coca-Cola.

The all-male regiment didn't always know what to make of her. She felt welcome to come into anyone's tent and make herself at home without being invited.

This type of text sets up a mystery. If students aren't predicting after reading this type of text, a simple question such as "Who do you think this might be?" will usually prompt predictions. Adding a metacognitive component would include asking: "In this text, I invited you to make predictions about who the newest Marine was. Do you think making predictions helped you understand the text? Did making predictions help you keep your mind on what you were reading? When might you use predictions again when you read?"

With these metacognitive prompts, we have done the following:

- Named the thinking that students were most likely using.
- Asked students to evaluate how effective the thinking was for them.
- Asked students if using this strategy or thinking helped them attend to the text. Sometimes we use strategies even when the text is simple and/or we fully understand the text. Strategy use helps us keep our focus on the text.
- Asked students to imagine when they might use this strategy again. We anticipate that students will struggle to answer this initially but over time, we want them to begin to understand that different strategies are sometimes suited to different types of texts. For examples, predictions are often helpful when there is a mystery or something to solve. They can also be helpful when coming up with an estimate answer for math (e.g., approximately what number should I get as an answer).

By the way, the new marine was a real-life character. She was named Reckless and she was a horse in the Korean conflict. She really did love to eat scrambled eggs and drink Coca-Cola! And she came into soldiers' tents so that she could stand by the wood burning stoves.

Teaching for understanding can and should include teaching comprehension strategies but modeling how to use a strategy is not enough. We need to invite students to think metacognitively and make decisions about when and what kind of strategy use helps them. We need to invite them to have conversations with one another about their use of strategies so that they understand how others think.

Consider what happens if a student answers that a strategy was not helpful. Such an answer provides a wonderful opportunity to talk about how people think differently about a text, as well as thinking metacognitively about strategies. Harvey and Goudvis (2017) offer a lovely lesson idea for evaluating connections to text and letting each students talk about if connections they made helped them understand the text or distracted them from thinking about what the text said.

One way to think about the different ways that just two people approach text is by imagining that two people walk into a special exhibit showcasing the art of Vincent van Gogh. One person knows very little about the artist but loves to paint for fun. The second person was an art major in college. The first person may try to understand the way van Gogh played with light in paintings and try to imagine how he would copy that use of light. The second person might look at the same painting and think about the history of van Gogh, including that he was in an asylum and suffered from paranoia. His paintings reflected periods when his mental health was deteriorating or was recovering. In both cases, the art observers are actively thinking about the paintings. However, their focus and thinking are very different. This helps explain why we can't simply sequence a list of strategies for instruction and expect students to practice and apply them equally.

One of the biggest challenges with teaching comprehension is that it is an internal process. We can't "see" comprehension. Further, that internal process varies from individual to individual. While we understand the larger patterns of the way people comprehend (often referred to as reading strategies), each person uses these strategies in unique combinations at specific times. This is one reason why attempts to specify a sequence for teaching comprehension strategies does not work in the same way that sequencing phonics instruction works.

What vocabulary should I teach?

We cannot teach every word that students will need to know in order to understand and communicate. Fisher and Frey (2020) recommended six considerations as a protocol for choosing words that are worth teaching.

- Representative: Does the word represent a concept, a family of words, or idea that is essential for understanding the larger whole?
- Repeatability: Will the word be used again in the text, the content, or the school year?
- Transportable: Will the word be used in discussion, writing, or other subject areas?
- Contextual Analysis: Can students use context clues to determine the word meaning without help?
- Structural Analysis: Can students use structural analysis of parts such as roots, prefixes, and suffixes to arrive at the definition without help?
- Cognitive Load: What is the cognitive load of this lesson and of the students' day? Are there already too many new words for students to learn in this lesson?

What makes a word "sticky" or memorable? Words that describe a single, concrete object (such as the word zarf) are stickier than words that describe abstract concepts (such as the word democracy). Our job is to make the words we choose to teach as sticky as possible. We do this by providing multiple exposures, offering multiple ways of encountering the word (not just visual but visual and auditory and kinetic when possible), and creating concrete scenarios for abstract concepts. If we really want to make the word sticky, we will need to give multiple ways or degrees of learning the word.

Degrees of Teaching Definitions

- Give an experience
- Add a visual
- Give an example
- Tell/show the definition

Telling students a definition is a lower degree of experiencing the word than giving the students an example. An example is a lower degree than an experience. Making a word sticky will include giving students all those degrees of word learning with a word whenever possible. For example, Ms. Tyson taught echolocation by first writing the definition of echolocation on the board, along with an example and a quick sketch of a bat and an insect. Next, she talked about the words echo and location that make up echolocation. Then, she had students perform a short word skit in which a few students acted out being the bats and the prey while she narrated. Students heard the word multiple times on the first day of the unit—but Ms. Tyson knew that her students still needed to experience the word over time. Across several days, her students read texts about echolocation. They used it in writing and speaking.

At this point, you might be saying that it seems like it would take a long time to provide all of this support. And you're right! That's why we need to be very thoughtful about what words students need to know at a Level 4—the highest level of understanding. We need to be purposeful about our vocabulary time and not assume that every word listed as a vocabulary word in a teacher's manual can be or should be taught to a Level 4.

We also need to be intentional about the vocabulary activities that we use. We love a fun activity as much as the next teacher. A variety of books and resources offer lists of 50 vocabulary activities or 20 vocabulary games. While these sources can be helpful to generate ideas, a random collection of activities will not help students achieve the deepest levels of word knowledge needed to understand dense material. Phillips et al. (2008) wrote:

> Unfortunately, too many teachers resort to copying definitions as the strategy of choice in vocabulary instruction. When asked why they use this method, teachers respond that it saves time and enables them to progress to the actual content in a more efficient manner. (p. 62)

Vocabulary research documents that the practice of copying definitions is not effective for helping students gain deep and lasting conceptual knowledge of words. Other ineffective practices include preteaching vocabulary before developing students' conceptual meaning resulting in rote memorization (Suárez & Gesa, 2019).

To avoid the random collection of vocabulary activities, we need an intentional plan for teaching vocabulary—one that is more detailed than seeing a word in a teacher's manual and giving students a quick definition or asking them to memorize the words. The plan should help students move through the levels of vocabulary knowledge. We recommend the following:

1. Determine what level of knowledge students need about each word. For example, students may need to know that oligarchy and monarchy are connected to the government but they don't need to use the words. They need familiarity but not deep knowledge. Oppositely, they may need a deeper understanding of the word representative which will require more exposures to the word and more opportunities for them to use the word.
2. Plan for multiple exposures across time.
3. Vary your vocabulary activities in a unit. Avoid having them write definitions or create vocabulary cards for every word. Instead, arrange the activities to help students move from a level one (or no knowledge of the word) to a level four (deep knowledge of the word) by starting with activities that help them associate the words with the correct concept. For example, a beginning vocabulary activity might include a vocabulary sort, followed by creating a visual with the words, and finally writing the word with synonyms and antonyms in a vocabulary notebook.
4. Create opportunities for students to use the words in speaking and writing.

Finally, because students enter school with a wide range of vocabulary sizes, we need to plan for differentiation. Sousa and Tomlinson (2011) distinguish between four different ways we can provide differentiated instruction: content differentiation, process differentiation, product differentiation, and environmental differentiation. Using text sets or collections allows us to offer content differentiation in vocabulary. While one group may be reading text A about bats and learning about echolocation with simplified language, another group may be reading text B about bats and encountering the same key word with more difficult language to match their reading needs. We offer process differentiation when we provide additional exposures to one group of students through additional text, time to talk, and opportunities to write. Product differentiation occurs when we have different expectations for how students show their knowledge of the vocabulary. Some students may be asked to give verbal responses while others are expected to give independent written responses. The environments that we create can be differentiated by providing a mix of individual, partner, small group, and whole group instruction.

We have included a more detailed vocabulary plan in Appendix B.

Partnering with families

Reading is very personal for many families. They want their children to be good readers. At the same time, they may be very worried about how their student is performing. Empathize with families' concerns about their child. Learning to read can be very emotional for families as well as children. Listen, take notes about your observations, and invite the families to document what they observe at home. Seek additional support from other professionals but try to avoid diagnoses of any type unless you are qualified to make specific diagnoses. As you seek more information and continue to assess each student, make sure the family has a concrete way to address vocabulary and comprehension at home. We like to begin with three invitations for families:

1. Learn something new as a family—and talk about it. Each new experience has new vocabulary and builds new background knowledge for future connections. For example, Dixie's family recently went snowshoeing for the first time. A few words we encountered were backcountry, designated trails, avalanche, and bindings. The experience doesn't have to be expensive—taking a walk in a new place can be an experience. The key is to talk about what you see, such as naming the plants and the birds, or using a field guide to model looking up names for the things that you see. Invite families to extend these initial connections by checking out a book at the library or watching a video. This allows for multiple exposures to words and concepts.
2. Write. The fact is that the school day often doesn't have enough time for students to write often or write about what interests them. Make sure that all students have access to materials to write by sending home quality writing materials. Encourage families to write at home about what they did or what they are reading. Literacy consists of reciprocal processes—reading and writing, speaking and listening. We can improve one part of the circuit by working on the other. Students can write mini-books about their new experiences or write a blog about their latest book. Encourage diagrams, images, and charts. Writing will give students a space to use the new vocabulary and collect what they know.
3. Talk. Watch a movie. Read. Play a video game. Participate in important cultural traditions. And then invite the student to talk about what they are thinking and why. Reading might be your ideal as the teacher, but even movies and video games can provide opportunities for families to invite students to summarize (what happened) and talk about what

they were thinking (Why did you think that would happen? Why did you make that decision?) This helps students be able to describe their thinking and begins the process of helping them think about their own thinking. For example, Dixie's children enjoyed playing Minecraft for several years. After sitting and watching for a few minutes, Dixie realized she had no idea why they were doing what they were doing. A few questions such as, "What made you decide to do that?" made Dixie realize there was a lot that she didn't know and that they were being very strategic in their decision-making. They were connecting to previous experiences playing the game (making connections), guessing where they would encounter opposition (predictions), and trying something different when their first plan didn't work (monitoring). All of those ways of thinking are useful in reading as well. Knowing when your students are using those kinds of thinking patterns and referencing them when reading together can help students understand more about how they think and how others think.

Ultimately, all reading instruction should help students comprehend and make sense of what they are reading, listening to, or viewing. Comprehension is the primary goal of reading.

Reflective questions

1. How would you explain what comprehension is? How do you recognize if a student has failed to comprehend what they read?

2. Prior knowledge is vital to both comprehension and vocabulary. Describe a time when prior knowledge helped you understand a text or task. Describe a time when prior knowledge interfered with your comprehension.

3. What do you remember about vocabulary instruction? What do you feel is essential to include in your own vocabulary plan?

References

Aukerman, M. (2008). In praise of wiggle room: Locating comprehension in unlikely places. *Language Arts*, 86(1), 52.

Biemiller, A., & Slonim, N. (2001). Estimating root word vocabulary growth in normative and advantaged populations: Evidence for a common sequence of vocabulary acquisition. *Journal of Educational Psychology, 93*(3), 498–520.
Castells, N., Minguela, M., Solé, M., Miras, M., Nadal, E., & Rijlaarsdam, G. (2021). Improving questioning-answering strategies in learning from multiple complementary texts: An intervention study. *Reading Research Quarterly, 57*(3), 879–912.
Dale, E., O'Rourke, J., & Bamman, H. (1971). *Techniques of teaching vocabulary.* Palo Alto, CA: Field Educational Publications.
Dean, J. (2015). *Pete the cat (series).* Scholastic.
Duffy, G. G. (2009). *Explaining reading: A resource for teaching concepts, skills, and strategies.* Guilford Press.
Elleman, A. M., & Oslund, E. L. (2019). Reading comprehension research: Implications for practice and policy. *Policy Insights from the Behavioral and Brain Sciences, 6*(1), 3–11.
Fisher, D., & Frey, N. (2020). *Improving adolescent literacy* (5th ed.). Pearson.
Guthrie, J. (2007). *Engaging adolescents in reading.* Corwin Press.
Harvey, S., & Goudvis, A. (2017). *Strategies that work: Teaching comprehension for understanding, engagement, and building knowledge, grades K-8.* Stenhouse Publishers.
Landauer, T. K., & Dumais, S. T. (1997). A solution to Plato's problem: The latent semantic analysis theory of acquisition, induction, and representation of knowledge. *Psychological review, 104*(2), 211.
Leslie, L., & Caldwell, J. (2021). *Qualitative reading inventory – 7.* Pearson.
Marzano, R. J. (2004). *Building background knowledge for academic achievement.* Alexandria, VA: Association for Supervision and Curriculum Development.
Pearson, P. D., & Cervetti, G. N. (2017). The roots of reading comprehension instruction. In S. E. Israel (Ed.), *Handbook of research on reading comprehension* (2nd ed., pp. 12–56). Routledge.
Pressley, M., & Afflerbach, P. (1995). *Verbal protocols of reading: The nature of constructively responsive reading.* Lawrence Erlbaum Associates.
Scott, J. A., Nagy, W. E., & Flinspach, S. L. (2008). More than merely words: Redefining vocabulary learning in a culturally and linguistically diverse society. In E. Farstrom & S. J. Samuels (Eds.), *What research has to say about vocabulary instruction* (pp. 182–210). International Reading Association.
Sousa, D. A., & Tomlinson, C. A. (2011). *Differentiation and the brain: How neuroscience supports the learner-friendly classroom.* Solution Tree Press.
Suárez, M. D. M., & Gesa, F. (2019). Learning vocabulary with the support of sustained exposure to captioned video: Do proficiency and aptitude make a difference?. *The Language Learning Journal, 47*(4), 497–517.
Wolf, M., & Potter, K. (2018). *Reader, come home: The reading brain in a digital world.* Harper.

· 10 ·

WHEN A STUDENT STARTS MIDDLE SCHOOL, NOW WHAT? (DISCIPLINARY LITERACY)

Ms. Johnson recently asked a 13-year-old boy in her class to show her his online searching process. Initially, the search proceeded as she expected. The boy quickly entered a question into the search box. But what happened next surprised her. The boy never actually opened links in his search results. He only took information from what appeared in the search result initial lines. Another middle school student proudly stated that he didn't know how to type because he only needed to use AI to find the answer or even do his work for him. These are some of the many issues that face many middle school students and their teachers. What's different about reading in middle school compared to reading in elementary school? And why is understanding both elementary and middle school reading benchmarks so important?

Research: Middle school reading

It is tempting to fall into negativity about literacy at the middle school level. For decades, researchers have documented the declining scores of late elementary and adolescent readers (Alvermann, 2001; Biancarosa & Snow, 2004). The National Assessment of Educational Progress (NAEP, 2022) reading assessment measures reading comprehension. According to the 2022 NAEP scores, both fourth and eighth graders' reading scores decreased by three points when compared with the 2019 scores. By eighth grade, the average reading score was lower than all the previous assessment years for the past 25 years. Reading scores decreased across all performance groups, including high and low performing students and 30% of eighth graders performed below the Basic level of proficiency. Based on this commonly reported information, the outlook can seem downright gloomy.

Literacy demands in middle school

Before we give in to hopelessness, consider that these scores reflect the impact of a global pandemic. Even without such mass disruption, adolescence is a time of great challenges when it comes to literacy demands. Consider a few of these increased demands:

- Disciplinary literacy demands: In middle school, students are asked to focus on specific disciplines such as science, social studies, math, and more. While elementary teachers introduced the subjects in general ways, students will encounter increasing complexity in the disciplines. Each discipline will bring unique literacy demands (Hinchman & O'Brien, 2019; Shanahan & Shanahan, 2008), including new ways of generating information from texts with an increasing technical vocabulary load, and new ways of communicating within the disciplines including writing (e.g., lab reports in science). Disciplinary learning can even include new ways of talking. Windschitl (2019) observed, "Within the context of schooling, conceptions of literacy are increasingly being associated with the capacity for learners to engage in disciplinary meaning making through face-to-face deliberation and dialogue" (p. 7).
- Disciplinary literacy demands are increasing with more difficult texts. Students are also being asked to read longer amounts of text. At the same time, students may experience more demands on their time both inside and outside of school, resulting in shorter amounts of time to read in a single instance. The result can be decreased stamina for reading (Hiebert, 2014; McVeigh, 2019).
- Students will be given more assignments to conduct research and utilize online sources. Researchers who study reading of online sources refer to this as unbounded reading. It is different from bounded reading in that no single person creates the same path through text. Consider what

would happen if three people were asked to research immigration in the US. Even though the topic is the same, each person will enter different search terms, use different search engines, pull up different results, and follow different links within those results. Reading in unbounded texts is not the same as reading in bounded texts (Afflerbach & Cho, 2011; Massey, 2012). Students may comprehend in one system but struggle to comprehend at the same level in the other system. Lawless and Schrader (2008) wrote:

> Citizens in the 21st century must not only know how to decode and comprehend information as they have in the past, but they are also now responsible for efficiently and effectively finding and evaluating information as well as quickly adapting goals in response to the complexities of the environment. (p. 268)

- Students in middle and high school must self-regulate their study habits. Unfortunately, many students have no idea how they might improve their studying (Miller et al., 2009). Because they are unable to self-regulate their study approaches, they may resort to asking teachers for simpler explanations and less work.

The good news is that we can help students improve their skills and strategies in each of these areas. If you are an elementary teacher, you can help prepare students for learning in the disciplines. Middle school teachers can address literacy demands with purposeful instruction.

But I'm an elementary teacher!

If you are an elementary teacher, you may be thinking that this chapter doesn't apply to you. Especially if you are teaching or plan to teach the primary grades, issues of middle school can seem secondary to helping students learn to read through letter knowledge and word identification. However, realize that you are creating the prior knowledge framework that students will need to reference. Imagine a middle schooler who has had no introduction to ideas such as the day and night with the earth's rotation or laws and citizenship. For successful learning, students need to be introduced to concepts early and keep encountering increasing complexity within those concepts. Standards such as the Common Core attempt to build in complexity across the grades. Consider the writing goals in Table 10.1.

In kindergarten, students are asked to use drawing, writing, or dictation to compose an opinion. By middle and high school, students are required to write

Table 10.1. Common Core Standards Writing Goals for Elementary

Grade	Standards
Kindergarten	• Use a combination of drawing, dictating, and writing to compose opinion pieces in which they tell a reader the topic or the name of the book they are writing about and state an opinion or preference about the topic or book. • Use a combination of drawing, dictating, and writing to compose informative/explanatory texts in which they name what they are writing about and supply some information about the topic. • Use a combination of drawing, dictating, and writing to narrate a single event or several loosely linked events. Tell about the events in the order in which they occurred, and provide a reaction to what happened. • Participate in shared research.
Second	• Write opinion pieces in which they introduce the topic or book they are writing about, state an opinion, supply reasons that support the opinion, use linking words (e.g., *because*, *and*, *also*) to connect opinion and reasons, and provide a concluding statement or section. • Write informative/explanatory texts in which they introduce a topic, use facts and definitions to develop points, and provide a concluding statement or section. • Write narratives in which they recount a well-elaborated event or short sequence of events, include details to describe actions, thoughts, and feelings, use temporal words to signal event order, and provide a sense of closure. • Participate in shared research.
Fourth and Fifth	• Write opinion pieces on topics or texts, supporting a point of view with reasons and information. • Write informative/explanatory texts to examine a topic and convey ideas and information clearly. • Write narratives to develop real or imagined experiences or events using effective technique, descriptive details, and clear event sequences. • Conduct short research projects.

Table 10.2. Common Core Standards Writing Goals for Middle and Secondary

Middle and High School	
Language Arts (Grades 6–12)	Social Studies/Science/Technical Subjects (Grades 6–12)
Write arguments to support claims using evidence	Write arguments focused on discipline-specific content.
Write informational texts to examine a topic with technical vocabulary, formal style	Write informative/explanatory texts, including the narration of historical events, scientific procedures/experiments, or technical processes.
Write narratives	Write narratives to develop real or imagined experiences or events using effective technique, relevant descriptive details, and well-structured event sequences.
Conduct research that draws on multiple sources	Conduct short research projects to answer a question (including a self-generated question), drawing on several sources and generating additional related, focused questions that allow for multiple avenues of exploration.

arguments to support claims using evidence in both language arts and the sciences. The work that the middle and high schoolers are doing is building on what they began in kindergarten.

Instruction

Elementary teachers

Even if you never teach middle school, you will play an important role in preparing your students for middle school. Four key practices are critical for helping students develop disciplinary reading habits.

Practice 1: Don't skip science and social studies

One of our teaching friends used the analogy of Swiss cheese to describe the gaps in students' learning. Like Swiss cheese in a sandwich, you know there are holes—you just don't know where they are. That is what middle school teachers can experience when students come to them with all different levels of science and social studies experiences. As elementary teachers, your job is to make those holes as small as possible, exposing your students to plenty of science and social studies concepts. We acknowledge how hard this practice can be. You will feel a great deal of pressure to cover a lot of information, to have your students reading at certain levels and performing in math at certain levels. Science and social studies frequently become the easiest things to cut from an already-packed day of instruction. But students are going to need the experiences from science and social studies. They will need the observation skills they practice by observing a cocoon. They will need the vocabulary that you discuss as you talk about rules and practice classroom voting.

Practice 2: Offer connected learning instead of single passages

Because the instructional days are so packed, many teachers we know try to integrate science and social studies into the reading curriculum. For example, the teacher asks the students to read a passage about photosynthesis and answer some comprehension questions. The next day, students might read about the Triangle Shirtwaist Factory Fire of 1911. Unfortunately, knowledge isn't built and maintained in this manner. Students need multiple exposures to connected ideas. Consider just the vocabulary load. If students see five brand-new words connected to photosynthesis and plants on day one, then see five more new words on the next day, and then move to a different topic on the third day, they have been exposed to 15 new words without any way to deepen their knowledge of those words and concepts. What happens for most students is that those words don't stick and if they encounter them again in another year, they may not even remember that they've seen those words. They need to spend multiple days on a connected topic so that they read, write, view, talk about, and experience things that are all connected to photosynthesis before moving on to a new topic.

When we were teaching elementary school, we would have responded, "When are we supposed to fit that in? My day is already packed!" Instead of trying to make big changes, target one small change you could make. For example, imagine that the upcoming science unit is about weather. You want to increase the time that students spend engaging in the content, but you simply don't have more minutes in the day. Consider replacing independent reading time with text sets in book bins that are placed on the students' tables.

Text sets are collections of texts created about a single overarching concept. Text sets offer a range of reading levels, a range of subtopics, and multiple genres. For example, a text set on weather could include printouts of the weather forecast for the last five years, books about weather, including unusual weather and weather-related jobs, a few fictional stories that feature weather, weather poems, and more. Many teachers already curate a collection of texts about a single topic and put the resources at the front of the room for students to peruse when they're done. If this is what you've observed or do, we encourage three small changes. First, put the books in book tubs that stay on the students' table groups so that they have easy access. After a few days or a week, rotate the tubs so that each group has access to a new set of texts. Second, make sure students have some time every day to access the texts instead of allowing access only for those who have free time. Third, create a way for students to share what they've learned. We like to have students write down something they learned, something that they think is interesting each time they read, or a question. When we are ready to focus on weather for our science time, we ask students to bring these statements and integrate them into the learning.

Practice 3: Read challenging texts

If possible, assign a section of a textbook or technical piece that is slightly above what most students in your class can read comfortably. This practice comes with a caution. Too much challenging text can be discouraging. At the same time, students need to know that they don't have to give up when they see a difficult text. Here are some tips for helping students read challenging text:

- Make sure that students have some background in the topic before reading the text so that some of the key vocabulary and concepts will be familiar.
- Affirm their value as readers. Explain that everyone may struggle when reading some texts and not being able to understand a text does not mean you are a bad reader.
- Model how to read a text more than once to get additional meaning.
- Model varying the rate that you read. If a text is more difficult, explain that they will need to slow their reading rate. Some students are used to reading fast and don't automatically vary their reading rate.
- Encourage students to focus on the big picture meaning of the reading by creating a "Big Picture" sentence. Allow students to share their sentences in partners and small groups. Encourage them to reread as a pair or group and see if they can add anything else to their Big Picture sentence.

Practice 4: Build morphemic awareness

Vocabulary is frequently the barrier between not understanding and understanding a text. And yet, as we covered in Chapter 9, we cannot teach all of the vocabulary that students will need to know. That means we have to focus on helping students be aware of meaningful parts of words. These meaningful parts, called morphemes, can help students generate their own word learning. For example, when students learn that -ology is a meaningful part and means the study of, they can generate a more accurate guess when they come to a word they have never seen that has -ology in it.

This is not always easy. In primary grades, students may have been asked to find small words they recognize inside a larger unknown word. Unfortunately, this process can become a barrier to students trying to use smaller words to figure out a definition. Consider a second grader who came to the word "selfish" and asked what the word was. When the teacher asked him if he saw any small words in selfish, he responded, "Fish!" He was correct. Fish is indeed a small word within selfish. Unfortunately, fish had nothing to do with the meaning of the word selfish.

As elementary teachers, you will be the first to teach students about meaningful word parts, from prefixes such as re- and dis- to simple root words such as bio- in biosphere or dict- in dictator or dictation.

For middle school teachers

It is important to continue the same practices that were started in elementary school, including reading challenging text and building awareness of morphemes and vocabulary. Table 10.3 summarizes some of the primary challenges for middle school readers, along with some suggestions for meeting those challenges. Additional attention should be given to support students' reading of Internet text, students' study and independent reading habits, and increasing students' reading stamina, study skills, and before self-regulation.

Table 10.3. Challenges of Middle School Literacy

Challenge	Instructional Response
The textbook is too difficult for students to read.	Do: Measure students' ability to read the text with accuracy. Provide opportunities to reread. Don't: Skip rereading challenging text.
Students do not attempt or complete homework.	Do: Teach study skills. Work towards self-regulation. Don't: Require every student to complete notetaking in the same way.
Reading Stamina.	Do: Help students explore their current stamina and what affects their stamina. Build stamina over time. Don't: Assign long readings that most students won't read or assign no readings at all.

Assessment

Continuing the assessment of cycle observation, conversation, artifacts/testing is important in middle school. Specific to middle school, we recommend using think alouds to better understand what students are thinking as they are reading. These are particularly helpful with older students who are able to narrate their thinking as they are completing a task. As with other observation and conversation assessments, we recommend starting with one or two focal students.

Adolescent Interview and Think Aloud

1. How would you describe yourself as a student?
2. How do you think your teachers would describe you as a student?
3. Are there classes and/or subjects at school that you are motivated to do well in? What are they and why are you motivated in these areas?
4. Are there things outside of school that you find motivating? Can you describe those?
5. Are there classes and/or subjects at school that you are not motivated to do well in? What are they?
6. Think about when you are motivated in school. Which of these statements describe what motivates you:
   - I like to learn new things
   - I like to get good grades
   - I have to do well to stay eligible for other activities
   - I like to make others (teachers, family) proud of me
7. If there are classes or subjects at school that you find motivating, what do the teachers do that help motivate you?
8. In the classes or subjects that aren't motivating, what do the teachers do that fail to motivate you?
9. What advice would you give to me if I'm trying to motivate students?

Digital reading

> Coiro et al. (2008) wrote:
> Literacy acquisition may be defined not by acquiring the ability to take advantage of the literacy potential inherent in any single, static, technology of literacy (e.g., traditional print technology) but rather by a larger mindset and the **ability to continuously adapt** [emphasis added] to the new literacies required by the new technologies that rapidly and continuously spread on the Internet. Moreover, since there will likely be more new technologies that any single person could hope to accommodate, literacy will also include knowing how and when to make wise decisions about which technologies and which forms and functions of literacy most support one's purposes. (p. 5)

Because our students are digital natives, we can make false assumptions about their proficiency using Internet text to find answers to their questions. Traditional literacy skills (e.g., decoding words, knowing vocabulary, reading fluently, and comprehending literal and inferential information) are no longer sufficient because the definition of what it means to be literate keeps evolving (Jenkins et al., 2006; Leu et al., 2015). Leu et al. (2015) emphasized, "We are unable to simply apply what we know about individual differences from offline reading to online reading; the two are not necessarily isomorphic" (p. 259).

What is the answer? As with every topic, we encourage the use of the assessment framework, beginning with observations and conversations. We find the added use of a think aloud very useful with upper elementary and middle school students because it gives us insight into what students are doing and thinking.

Digital Literacy Questions with Think Aloud

Ask the student to search a topic, preferably one that is interesting to them. Ask them to think aloud about what they searched, how they entered the search terms, how they chose what links to click, etc. The goal is to understand more about how students choose to learn AND how they use the digital platforms compared to how they read traditional text.

1. Talk me through a typical search. What do you do first? How do you decide what to click?

2. What do you read on the Internet and in social media (think about blogs, memes, Instagram)?
3. Do you think your reading on the Internet is like or not like your reading of a traditional printed text? Describe.

Students need more skill accessing and creating their own textual trail in open, online environments. Kohnen and Saul (2018) summarized the issue this way:

> Many students work in schools inside a bubble of controlled or protected information. Instead of teaching students to attend to information from the outside world as an adult would or even talking about the information encountered in students' day-to-day lives, teachers and curriculum developers pretend that by managing, controlling, and approving of what students read and write in school, they are teaching them to become better adult readers and writers. In this bubble, students may be asked to engage with intellectually stimulating topics and might even emerge ready for college classwork, but they are often unprepared for the nonfiction demands of adult life. (p. 671)

One promising approach is CAPES (Context, Actions, Produces, Evaluate, Standards) (Coiro & Putman, 2014) which combines reading strategy use, Internet inquiry, and self-regulated behaviors. CAPES builds on research suggesting that Internet text requires the reader to use both foundational and additional reading strategies for comprehension (Pressley & Afflerbach, 1995; Afflerbach & Cho, 2011). These additional reading strategies include locating information, evaluating relevance of information, synthesizing information, and communicating information within digital formats. Cognitive and metacognitive strategies are managed by self-regulating strategies, including planning, acting, and reflecting. Coiro and Putman (2014) specified that while the cognitive and metacognitive reading strategies are important, they may not be enough to keep readers from being overwhelmed when doing Internet research, resulting in further de-motivation and lack of self-efficacy and persistence. To support the motivation and abilities to conduct Internet research, Coiro and Putman's CAPES model utilized teacher think alouds to help students understand how to read and evaluate Internet sources. Additionally, the teacher provides feedback, filling in the feedback loop until students are able to work collectively and ultimately independently to take responsibility for the cognitive and regulatory work. Once students become familiar with the cognitive, metacognitive, and regulatory strategies within the model, the CAPES approach is designed to be utilized independently or in small groups.

Stamina

Reading stamina is an issue challenging many students and teachers. Students may exhibit many maladaptive behaviors, including avoidance, distractibility, and excessive help-seeking. Teachers may find themselves faced with students who cannot read more than five minutes before seeking some other stimulation. The following areas can be helpful to consider.

Evaluate reading difficulty

Is the textbook too difficult for students to sustain independent reading? Measure this by checking in with two or three students that are frequently off-task when reading is assigned in class. Choose a passage (between 100 and 300 words is ideal) that the students have not read. Ask one student at a time to read to you. Take a running record if you are familiar with this kind of tracking. If not, simply make a tally for every word the student misses or reads incorrectly. At the end of the passage, ask the student to tell you the important ideas from the text that they would share with someone who had never read the passage.

Determine the percentage by dividing the number of words read correctly by the number of words in the passage. For example, if the student missed 15 words of a 300 word passage, the percentage would be found as follows:

$$300 - 15 = 285$$

$$285 \div 300 = 95\%$$

The 95% is the accuracy rating. There are many cut-off scores, but we suggest that anything below 90% will mean that the student is likely to struggle with independent reading of that specific text. Check by evaluating their summary statements. Image a student scored an 86% accuracy rating. He may still identify important information in the passage. He may also be able to handle the text independently but he may tire quickly because of all of the cognitive energy needed to decode and identify meaning.

If the focal students of this type of assessment all score below the 90% mark, it doesn't mean that you should not assign the text. In fact, they need to continue to practice reading text rather than having the content given to them in presentation or video format. It does mean that you will need to support them by building prior knowledge and vocabulary before assigning the text. It also means that you will need to plan to assign shorter segments of text because of the attention it will require.

Value rereading

Sometimes students assume that if they don't understand a text in the first reading, they must be a bad reader. We need to affirm that everyone struggles to read some text and all of us must reread some texts in order to better understand them.

Some students tell us they already reread and it doesn't help. We recommend spending time with these students and asking them to think aloud as they reread. One common pattern is that students read, realize that they don't understand, and go back to the beginning of the text, chapter, or section instead of identifying where their understanding broke down and focusing their attention there. In other words, they start over and reread in the same way that they read the first time. They may be unaware of how to read differently. Modeling how to pause and create mini-summaries, look up a definition, rephrase in one's own words, or translate a section into a chart or visual can be helpful.

Another common response from students is that rereading is boring. Rather than arguing with them, we ask them to practice a rereading format. Gallagher (2004) implemented First Draft and Second Draft readings. In First Draft reading, Gallagher asked his students to read for the big idea and answer the question, "What is this about?" Second Draft reading is key to moving beyond surface-level understanding. Gallagher summarized these with two additional questions: "What does it mean?" and "What does it matter?" (p. 85). Other rereading formats ask them to annotate the text and work collaboratively. The key is that students should be rereading for different and deeper purposes with each reading instead of merely rereading the passage for the same information.

Build stamina over time

Stamina is like a muscle and just like a muscle, the best way to build it is through consistent exercise that gradually increases in length and intensity. And just like any good physical trainer knows, berating a person for where he is at currently is more likely to alienate than encourage. In other words, help students understand their current level of reading stamina and encourage them to get stronger.

Assign students a text that they have not read and explain that you are curious how they would rate their current reading stamina. Add a level of seriousness by asking them to be ready to write a short summary of what they read. Display a timer so everyone can track their time spent reading. Have everyone begin reading and ask them to write down the time when they feel like they were restless to the point of losing their understanding.

This isn't a perfect measure by any means, but it does help draw students' attention to their own reading stamina. It is a good idea to assign reading during other times and use observation to track which students get up or seem distracted in one minute intervals. Additionally, keep in mind that stamina is not something that one has or doesn't have. It can be influenced by genre, interest, and personal circumstances. Involve students in describing their reading stamina through self-reflection.

Once students have a sense of how long they can read before they begin to lose comprehension and begin to get distracted, talk about setting personal goals for increasing reading stamina. This is incremental. Someone who sits on the couch may want to run a 5K within a week of starting an exercise program, but the reality is that it takes weeks of consistent work. Similarly, reading stamina can be built, but it takes consistent attention and work.

Teach study habits

Study habits are an important component of stamina. If students don't know how to read and reread with a purpose or how to organize information, they are more likely to lack focus. As a result, they may struggle with stamina for reading and for homework. We recommend focusing on the following areas:

- organizational skills: How do they keep information so that they can retrieve it?
- annotating skills: How do they mark text to identify important information and help stay connected to the text?
- note-taking skills: How do they take notes in a way that identifies important information and not simply copy information?
- time-management skills: How do they manage time for studying? How do they break down large multi-day assignments?

It is important to model each of these areas. After students learn the initial method, allow them to choose what works best for them.

Miller et al. (2009) worked with students and teachers to identify current habits and set goals for future grades. They interviewed students about their current grades in a science class and confirmed this with teacher records. Next, they asked students what grade they hoped to get and how they planned to ensure they were prepared for weekly quizzes. Then, they asked students to describe their study habits. After the quizzes, students were again interviewed about their quiz grade and if their grade matched their predicted grade. If the quiz grade did not match the predicted grade, the interviewers and students discussed changes that they might implement. For some, this included minimizing distractions (e.g., turning off the tv or silencing the phone). Some needed to take notes. Others needed more effective ways to study their notes. The bottom line was that students often lacked the skills necessary to study for quizzes because they were used to teachers reading information to them or providing study guides that matched the tests.

Even for those who do not plan on teaching middle school, it is important to think about the ways in which older students access literacy. Literacy at the middle school level requires that students are able to read and comprehend in different disciplines where the vocabulary and language may differ. Providing instruction that supports stamina to read longer text and clarity about how to locate information digitally is beneficial for all ages.

Reflective questions

1. Review the information from the writing standards across the grades in Tables 10.1 and 10.2. What differences do you notice? What similarities do you notice? Did anything surprise you?

2. This chapter suggests that elementary teachers use a series of passages or texts that are connected to a single topic in order to build conceptual knowledge. Connected information may not be provided by a curriculum. What opportunities for extending reading within certain subjects can you offer to students?

3. What have you observed about stamina for reading in classrooms you've visited? Do you think reading stamina is increasing or decreasing? What ideas do you have for increasing stamina for reading in your classroom?

References

Afflerbach, P. P., & Cho, B. Y. (2011). The classroom assessment of reading. In M. Kamil, P. D. Pearson, E. Moje, & P. Afflerbach (Eds.), *Handbook of reading research-IV* (pp. 487–514). Routledge.

Alvermann, D. E. (2001). Reading adolescents' reading identities: Looking back to see ahead. *Journal of Adolescent & Adult Literacy*, 44(8), 676–690.

Biancarosa, G., & Snow, C. E. (2004). *Reading next: A vision for action and research in middle and high school literacy: A report from Carnegie Corporation of New York*. Alliance for Excellent Education.

Coiro, J., & Putman, M. (2014). Teaching students to self-regulate during online inquiry (IRA E-ssentials series). Retrieved from https://www.literacyworldwide.org/docs/default-source/member-benefits/e-ssentials/ila-e-ssentials-8049.pdf

Coiro, J., Knobel, M., Lankshear, C., & Leu, D. J. (2008). Central issues in new literacies and new literacies research. In J. Coiro, M. Knobel, C. Lankshear, & D. J. Leu (Eds.), *Handbook of research on new literacies* (pp. 1–22). Routledge.

Gallagher, K. (2004). *Deeper Reading*. Stenhouse.

Hiebert, E. H. (2014). The forgotten reading proficiency: Stamina in silent reading.. Retrieved from https://textproject.org/wp-content/uploads/2022/07/Hiebert-2015.pdf

Hinchman, K. A., & O'Brien, D. G. (2019). Disciplinary literacy: From infusion to hybridity. *Journal of Literacy Research*, 51(4), 525–536.

Jenkins, H., Clinton, K., Purushotma, R., Robinson, A. J., & Weigel, M. (2006). *Confronting the challenges of participatory culture: Media education for the 21st century*. MacArthur Foundation.

Kohnen, A. M., & Saul, E. W. (2018). Information literacy in the internet age: Making space for students' intentional and incidental knowledge. *Journal of Adolescent & Adult Literacy*, 61(6), 671–679.

Lawless, K., & Schrader, P. G. (2008). Where do we go now?. In J. Coiro, M. Knobel, C. Lankshear, & D. Leu (Eds.), *Handbook of research on new literacies* (pp. 267–296). Routledge.

Leu, D. J., Kiili, C., & Forzani, E. (2015). Individual differences in the new literacies of online research and comprehension. In P. Afflerbach (Ed.), *Handbook of individual differences in reading* (pp. 277–290). Routledge.

Massey, D. D. (2012). Differentiating instruction for adult learners in an online environment. In R. Hartshorne & T. Heafner (Eds.), *Teacher education programs and online learning tools: Innovations in teacher preparation*. IGI Global.

Miller, S. D., Heafner, T. L., & Massey, D. D. (2009). High-school teachers' attempts to promote self-regulated learning: I may learn from you, yet how do I do it? *The Urban Review*, 41. 121–140.

McVeigh, F. (2019). *Creating passionate readers through independent reading. Literacy leadership brief.* International Literacy Association.

NAEP. (2022). *NAEP report card: 2022 NAEP reading assessment.* Retrieved from https://www.nationsreportcard.gov/highlights/reading/2022/

Pressley, M., & Afflerbach, P. (1995). *Verbal protocols of reading: The nature of constructively responsive reading.* Lawrence Erlbaum Associates.

Shanahan, T., & Shanahan, C. (2008). Teaching disciplinary literacy to adolescents: Rethinking content-area literacy. *Harvard Educational Review, 78*(1), 40–59.

Windschitl, M. (2019). Disciplinary literacy versus doing school. *Journal of Adolescent & Adult Literacy, 63*(1), 7–13.

CONCLUSION

Invitations to families and teachers

Throughout this book, we summarized research and theories and shared instructional approaches to help students overcome reading challenges. We emphasized that as reading teachers, we must look at our instruction in relation to the reader, text, task, and context. We highlighted the role of assessment in understanding how to address and overcome reading difficulties we see in children. We also viewed parents as partners in this process. Crisis narratives about students who are not reading or reading below benchmark grade level can start very early. Our role as educators is to work adaptively to support students in overcoming the reading challenges they may experience.

Planning with families

Overcoming reading challenges requires targeted instructional approaches in school, but we cannot rely on school instruction alone. The need to work with families is vital when working with students to support reading development and achievement. We recommend the following:

- Listen to families. Invite students and their families to share stories about their child and also about their experiences as readers.
- Be aware that not all families will feel comfortable at school. When appropriate, visit families at home. Facilitate participation by sending home materials and books to families.
- When you do talk, be sure to affirm the child and their family. Every conversation shouldn't be about the concerns.
- Focus on reading as a whole. Try to include the constrained skills (letter recognition, decoding, fluency) as well as the unconstrained skills (comprehension, reading authentic stories for enjoyment). If we focus too much on the parts of reading at the neglect of the purposes of reading (understanding and enjoyment), we risk creating a motivation problem. In other words, if a child needs work on decoding, they will benefit from explicit decoding instruction (the parts), but they also need to see words in context, enjoy listening to stories, and practice thinking (the whole).
- Have a plan. We don't mean Individualized Education Plans, though that might be the end step. Instead, show parents and guardians that you are monitoring their student's growth. The plan should include what you will do and a timeframe, as well as what families can do at home to support shared goals. Invite conversations with families about the plan. Remember that parents and guardians are their child's first teacher.

A sample plan might include waiting for four weeks before giving a decoding test again. In that time, the child will be part of a small group that focuses on letter recognition and decoding work. They will also be listening to meaningful stories during whole group instruction and invited to spend independent reading time rereading familiar stories as well as using visually-supported texts such as wordless books so that they can continue to practice making meaning from texts on their own. Invite the family to focus on reading meaningful stories at home, listening to audiobooks, talking with elders to hear stories, and playing with words through silly rhymes, poems, songs, etc.

Demystifying reading

As you plan with families, demystify the process of reading in school. Avoid educational jargon and terms that may be unfamiliar some terms to explain include:

1. Testing and curriculum terms: When talking about comprehension, it is common to use terms that are associated with the particular tests that are administered in your school and state. Terms like AYP, close reading, benchmark, and even standards can be confusing to families. Remember that these are specialized vocabulary words that although are familiar to school personnel might be unfamiliar to others. Try to talk about how a student is doing through a series of positive, straightforward statements that offer the next action step. For example, you might say, "(Student's name) identifies words very well. In class, we are working to stop at the end of a page and think about what happened. You can model this at home, with movies or books by pausing and stating what has happened so far."
2. Your school may use terms such as Tier 1, Tier 2, and Tier 3 to describe vocabulary words for instructional supports for students. Be sure to provide a diagram and/or explanation of these words to families.
3. Metacognition is critical to comprehension, yet families might not have encountered this word (we didn't until we went to graduate school). Sharing the components of the word (meta and cognition) may only result in a vague idea of what the word means as it connects to literacy instruction. A simple question such as, "What do you do if you are reading something, and it doesn't make sense?" can help clarify what this term means and why it is so important for instruction.

Throughout this book, we provide concrete explanations of reading terms. We encourage you to share the definition of these terms as outlined in the text with parents and guardians.

Middle school families

Being a caregiver is hard. Hearing that a child is not reading where they should brings out a lot of fears for families. The families may fear they aren't good enough, their child will never recover, and more. This is true for all grades and ages but especially as students enter middle school. Parents are not asked to participate in reading homework in the same way that they were in elementary school years. Students may change their reading habits. This can leave families uncertain as to how to help their middle school students. We encourage families to support middle schoolers in three ways:

- Access: Look for opportunities to give students access to texts while allowing them to change the kinds of texts they like to read. This might include visiting bookstores and used bookstores, allowing them to download their local library's platform for online books, or gifting them a subscription to audiobooks.
- Conversations: Conversations are sometimes difficult with middle school students. They may be more interested in communicating with friends. Encourage parents to do all they can to continue conversation by asking questions about their student's interests and preferences. Questions to suggest are: "Do you prefer listening to an audiobook or reading the book in print?" "Do you prefer to read from a screen or from a printed page?" "Do you think teachers should still assign reading or should you be able to learn from Youtube?" These kinds of questions provide insight into students' thinking and their changing opinions and identities.
- Experiences: When children were young, families might have enjoyed simple experiences to both entertain and teach students such as walks in the park, trips to a zoo, or visiting a nature center. Students will still benefit from fun experiences that still connect them to science, social studies, and math content. For example, a ghost tour of a local historical site provides background knowledge of an important historical place and time period and can spark interest.

Invitations to teachers

We want to emphasize that reading and teaching reading is complex. One of our favorite teachers of all time, Dr. Gerald Duffy equated teaching with the art of balancing roundstones (Duffy, 1998). It requires careful precision, knowledge of research and theories as well as instructional strategies and skills, creativity, compassion, ongoing learning, and more.

Just as we noted that building reading stamina takes time, growing as a teacher takes time. It does not happen all at once. Engage in careful reflection of your practices and your vision. Model learning and problem-posing and questioning. Continually reflect on your vision for teaching reading and ask your students what they think, what they want to know, and plan alongside your students, their families, and colleagues. And remember that you are in the best profession there is!

Reference

Duffy, G. G. (1998). Teaching and the balancing of round stones. *Phi Delta Kappan*, 79(10), 777–780.

Appendix A
STUDENT INTERVIEWS

Primary grades

1. Do you think reading is important? Why or why not?
2. Do you prefer to have a book read aloud to you or to read a book to yourself?
3. What kinds of books do you enjoy?
4. What's hardest about reading? What's easiest?
5. How do you feel about reading a book in your free time?
6. What do you think you need to do to become a better reader?

Intermediate grades

1. How much reading have you done in the past week? PROMPT: Does that include reading texts, email, or other social media? If not, how much do you think you read including social media?
2. Have teachers done anything that made you interested in reading a certain book? What was it?
3. Have you read something that was so memorable that you keep thinking about it or you told someone else about it?
4. Do you talk with anyone about the books you read? Who do you talk to, and what kinds of things do you talk about?
5. What's hardest about reading? What's easiest?
6. What do you think you need to do to become a better reader?

Appendix B
VOCABULARY PLAN

Our goal for teaching vocabulary is to move students through the levels of knowledge while building increasingly complex word and concept knowledge. Students need multiple exposures to the same words to move through the levels of vocabulary knowledge. Stahl and Nagy (2006) estimated that students need a minimum of four to twelve interactions with words, depending on many factors such as conceptual knowledge, understanding of roots and word part meanings, and interest. Multilingual Learners may need even more exposures to be able to connect it with other background knowledge, requiring multiple opportunities to interact with the word in context. Such ongoing exposure requires planning and purpose. Here we offer a model plan to structure vocabulary exposures.

Step One: Focus on broad conceptual association.

Focusing on broad conceptual association means (a) finding out what students know and (b) building a sense of the overall concept or topic.

To find out what students know, create an opportunity for students to talk and listen to their conversations. Ms. Graves asked her students to watch a short video showing an oil spill and then talk about what they saw. She wrote down phrases she overheard as she monitored student groups. Group 1 used the word pollution in reference to an oil spill, indicating that they were already thinking about the impact of oil spills. Group 2 used the word environment.

To honor student talk and begin to build an overall concept or map of the topic, Ms. Graves chose some of the key words from the students' conversations to write on the board. She knew students would encounter these words throughout the unit. She then used these two words as anchor words to create a word map. She put the environment in the circle, then began drawing lines connecting to the circle and writing new words on the lines. This reference chart remained visible throughout the lesson. It was revised twice. As students learned more, they regrouped the words that had been added to the chart.

Step Two: Move to categorization.

Step two in the vocabulary plan is to help students create more nuanced understandings of what the concept is and is not. In the example of renewable energy, we want students to be able to categorize and distinguish between renewable energy vs. nonrenewable energy. These categories provide the frame or the schema where individual words can be associated. Concept Sort are excellent ways to help students categorize their knowledge (Bear et al., 2007). They also serve to determine what students know before they start deeper exploration. For example, students can be given words prior to the reading and experiences and asked to sort them into two categories: renewable energy and nonrenewable energy.

Step Three: Include examples, nonexamples, and novel cases.

This component of a systematic plan is best combined with sorting. The emphasis is to help students develop a more nuanced understanding for what something is by learning more about what it is not. To accomplish this, we help students revisit the Concept Sort activities as they read, view, or do. Rather than telling students the correct answers after they have sorted, students are

Table B.1. Renewable and Nonrenewable Energy Concept Sort

Wind	Sun	Coal
Oil	Sustainable	Natural gas
Unlimited supply	Limited supply	Hydro/water
Geothermal	Fossil fuels	Combustible

asked to read or view a source and then adjust their sort based on the new information.

We may also highlight unusual cases, these become novel examples that serve as motivating hooks, authentic opportunities for students to ask questions, and evidence of complexity. We dig deeper into some of the words from the concept sort. For example, we highlight the concepts and words of renewable and recyclable by showing students a photo of a blade from a wind turbine being taken to the landfill. This allows us to discuss how wind turbines are used to capture wind and turn it into electricity, which is renewable energy. However, many parts of wind turbines are not recyclable or simply aren't recycled and end up in landfills.

Step Four: Create a reusable system for holding vocabulary thinking.

We love words. We love new words. Over and over, we've told ourselves we will remember a word only to forget not only what the word means, but what the actual word was. Students encounter hundreds of new words over the course of a few weeks. Thus, if we do not help them 'hold' the words, most words will be lost. That is why developing a system for holding the words is crucial. Some teachers use notecards. Other teachers have students create a section for vocabulary in their science notebooks. A word sort can be written in a notebook and students cross through words and move them to a new category in different colors of pencils. This allows them to see what they thought and how their thinking has changed. Ms. Webb frequently asked students to look back at their notebooks and find a place that their thinking changed and explain why.

Step Five: Review.

At this point in the plan, we begin to incorporate an intentional focus on multiple exposures through games such as *I'm Thinking of a Word*. The teacher begins by saying, "I'm thinking of a word. It has a suffix that means 'capable or worthy of.'" Additional clues are given until students can guess "sustainable."

INDEX

A

academic tasks 17
aggressive practices 5
Allington, R. L. 4, 29, 30
alphabetic principle 6
annotating skills 140
assessment
   artifacts and testing 47–8
   constrained skills 42–3
   conversations and interviews 45–7
   family involvement 49–50
   formative 40
   framework 42
   influences on skills 43–4
   information management 48–9
   level 1/below proficiency 40
   observation 44–5
   strengths-based 40
   vs. testing 40–2
   unconstrained skills 43
authentic tasks 17

B

background knowledge 113–15
balance student choice and teacher voice 61
bead slides 101
benchmarks for reading
   alphabetic principle 6
   decoding 6
   defined 5–6
   parents, role of 10–11
   phonological awareness 6
   reading instruction guidelines 9–10
Black, P. 40
books to discuss agency 78
books to teach skills 91
broad conceptual association 153–4
Brown Bear, Brown Bear (pattern book) 18

C

The Café method 31

Cervetti, G. N. 109
Chall, J. S. 65
Chard, D. J. 98
child-as-an-active-learner 15
Coiro, J. 136, 137
Common Core State Standards 5, 20
common vowel patterns 100
communicative tasks 17
community participation 57
comprehension 4, 8, 16, 108
comprehension strategies 34, 108
conceptual knowledge 113–15
constrained skills 42–3
Context, Actions, Produces, Evaluate, Standards (CAPES) 137
contexts 19–20
conversations and interviews 45–7
critical reflection 34–6
Csikszentmihalyi, M. 60
cultivate curiosity 62–3
culturally responsive teaching 27–8
The Curious Classroom (book) 63
curricular texts 18

D

The Daily Five 30–1
Daniels, H. 63
decodable texts 17–18
decoding 6
   assessments 103–5
   defined 97
   instruction on 99–102
developmental perspectives
   categories 14, 15
   contexts 19–20
   readers 14–15, 19
   tasks 16–17, 19
   texts 17–19
Developmental Reading Assessment 6
Duffy, G. G. 148

E

effective reading 28–30
elementary reading attitude survey 59
elementary teachers
   challenging texts 133
   common core standards writing goals 130
   morphemic awareness 133–4
   single passages 132–3
   skipping science and social studies 131–2
equitable reading instruction
   The Café method 31
   classroom learning 27
   common difficulties 36
   culturally responsive teaching 27–8
   The Daily Five 30–1
   effective reading 28–30
   Ms. Hatkes Center Chart 29
   workshop approach 30
   see also visioning
evaluation of motivation 64
explicit teaching of targeted skills 89
expository texts 18
external barriers 76

F

families, planning with 145–6
family involvement 49–50
First Grade Reading Vision 75
Fisher, D. 120
fluency 4, 8
   assessments 103–5
   components of 99
   defined 97
   instruction on 102–3
   National Reading Panel 98
fluent readers 105
formative assessment 40
Frey, N. 120

G

Gallagher, K. 139
Gambrell, Linda 71
games and activities 101
Goudvis, A. 119
Grandin, Temple (*The Autistic Brain*) 21
Griffith, L. W. 98
Griffith-Ross, D. A. 98

H

Harvey, S. 119

I

interactive read alouds 90
intermediate grades 151–2
internal barriers 76
International Literacy Association 16

J

Johnston, P. H. 66

K

Kohnen, A. M. 137

L

Lawless, K. 129
letter and word relationships 90
Leu, D. J. 136
leveled texts 18
Lunch Lady (trade book) 18

M

Massey, D. D. 62, 67
metalinguistic awareness 87
middle schoolers 71
middle school families 147–8
middle school reading
    common core standards writing
        goals 130, 131
    disciplinary literacy demands 128
    online sources 128–9
    students in 129
middle school teachers
    assessment 135
    challenges of 134
    digital reading 136
    reading difficulty evaluation 138–9
    reading stamina 138–40
    study habits 140–1
    value rereading 139
Miller, S. D. 62, 66, 67, 141
motivation
    ABCDEs of instruction 58
    ability 56–7
    assess 58–9
    balance student choice and teacher
        voice 61
    community participation 57
    cultivate curiosity 62–3
    data points 59
    description 55
    elementary reading attitude survey 59
    evaluation 64
    expectancy 56
    interviews 60–1
    observations 59
    reading in school challenges 57
    read profile-revised 60
    social competence 64
    systematic plans 58
    tasks 62

text choices 61–2
value 56
Ms. Hatkes Center Chart 29
multilingual learners 153
multimodal learning 79

N

NAEP Fluency Scale 104
narrative texts 18
National Assessment of Educational
  Progress (NAEP) 127–8
National Governors Association Center
  for Best Practices & Council of Chief
  State School Officers 5
The National Reading Panel
  (2000) 4, 16
National Research Council 4
Neuman, S. B. 41
The New Marine 117–18
No Child Left Behind Act
  (NCLB) 4
note-taking skills 140

O

Observation Protocol 45
online texts 19
organizational skills 140

P

pattern texts 18
Pearson, P. D. 109
Pete the Cat series 107
phoneme 86
phonemic awareness 4
  defined 86–7
  early literacy skills 92
  forms of assessment 93–4
  importance of 88–9
  instructional approaches 89–91
  metalinguistic 87
  ongoing monitoring and assessing
    children 91
  partnering with families 94–5
  phoneme 86
  phonological 87
  relationship of terms 85, 86
  transfer of skills 92–3
phonics instruction 4
phonological awareness 6, 87
Pikulski, J. J. 98
poetic texts 18
Pressley, M. 28
primary grades 151
project based learning 78
Putman, M. 137

R

RAND Reading Study Group 14
Rasinski, T. V. 98
readers 14–15
reader's experiences 108
reading comprehension
  artifacts/testing 112–13
  author and text 109
  conversation 111–12
  flowchart 116
  observation protocol 110, 111
  partnering with families 123–4
  reader's experiences 108
  text structure 117
  ways of thinking 108–9
Reading First Initiative, defined 4
reading materials 101
reading process 146–7
receptive and communicative
  processes 16
renewable and nonrenewable energy
  concept sort 154
role of assessment 7–9

S

sample picture books 34
Saul, E. W. 137
Schrader, P. G. 129
scientifically-based reliable reading research 4
Scott, J. A. 109
Seventh Grade Reading Notebook 74
social competence 64
sound-letter relationships 100
Sousa, D. A. 122
Spear-Swerling, L. 21
Stahl, K. 153
standards of reading
    Fifth grade 20
    Kindergarten 20
    Third grade 20
strengths-based assessment 40
student agency
    defined 71
    dispositional 73
    effective reading teachers 72
    external barriers 76
    instructional approaches 77–8
    internal barriers 76
    motivational 74–5
    multimodal learning 79
    parents support 79–80
    positional 75
    problems of 76–7
    project based learning 78
    support in classroom 72
student expectations 3
study habits 140–1
systematic plans 58

T

tactile activities 101
tasks 16–17, 19, 62
tasks of reading 16
teachers 22–3, 148
text choices 61–2
texts 17–19
time-management skills 140
Tomlinson, C. A. 122
topic baskets 29
trade books 18

U

unconstrained skills 43

V

value rereading 139
visioning
    defined 31–2
    development of 32
    sample statements 32–5
vocabulary 4, 8
    artifacts/testing 112–13
    component of comprehension 109
    conceptual and background knowledge 113–15
    conversation 111–12
    observation protocol 110, 111
    protocols 120
    research documents 121–2

W

Walczyk, J. J. 98
ways of thinking 108–9, 116
Wiliam, D. 40
word sorts 90

X

Xu, F. 15

www.ingramcontent.com/pod-product-compliance
Lightning Source LLC
Chambersburg PA
CBHW061716300426
44115CB00014B/2717